CAT
MAGIC

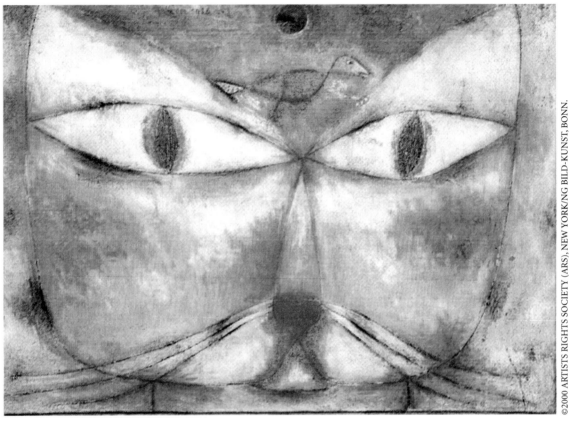

CAT MAGIC

Mews, Myths, and Mystery

PATRICIA TELESCO

Destiny Books
Rochester, Vermont

Destiny Books
One Park Street
Rochester, Vermont 05767
www.InnerTraditions.com

Destiny Books is a division of Inner Traditions International

Library of Congress Cataloging-in-Publication Data

Telesco, Patricia, 1960–
    Cat magic : mews, myths, and mystery / Patricia Telesco.
        p.   cm.
    ISBN 0-89281-774-7 (alk. paper)
    1. Cats—Miscellanea. 2. Cats—Mythology. 3. Magic. I. Title.
    BF1623.A33T45   1999
    398'.3699752—dc21   99-37550
                                             CIP

Printed and bound in Italy

10 9 8 7 6 5 4 3 2

Text design and layout by Kristin Camp

This book was typeset in Minion with Trajan as the display typeface

Frontispiece: Paul Klee, Cat and Bird *(private collection).*

CONTENTS

SIX

THE PURRFECT PET   128

Let Hercules himself do what he may
the cat will mew
and the dog will have his day
SHAKESPEARE

INTRODUCTION

Who is to bell the cat?
AESOP

Cats. In Germany people call them *ket,* in Ireland, *cait,* in Arabia, *quttah,* and in Scotland, *catti.* By any name, cats have scurried into almost every corner of human history and society, from the simple to the sublime. In Egypt, cats were

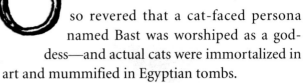

so revered that a cat-faced persona named Bast was worshiped as a goddess—and actual cats were immortalized in art and mummified in Egyptian tombs.

Reverence toward cats was not a localized phenomenon by any means. Greek art connects cats to the moon goddess Diana, and Scandinavians dedicate them to Freyja, a goddess of the night whose cart is drawn by cats. The Muslims even consider cats blessed creatures.

Romans depicted pet cats in their art, and ancient naturalists such as Pliny wrote extensively about this animal's hunting skills. Later we find cats as shipmates on boats to the New World, keeping the vessels free of disease-carrying mice. Cats also participate in marvelous folktales, such as that of the Pied Piper, and in classic writings, for example, the Cheshire Cat in Lewis Carroll's *Alice in Wonderland*.

Today, cats show up in casual conversation all the time. For example, if a cat has not "got your tongue," you could find yourself "letting the cat out of the bag." When tired, you may want to take a catnap. Children read Dr. Seuss's *Cat in the Hat*, play cat's cradle, and might caterwaul if they tangle the string.

Besides all this pussyfooting around, an entire industry has grown around these household pets. Cat litter was invented in the late 1940s and became a multimillion-dollar business. Magazines dedicate their pages to feline faces, and more than 600 cat

Opposite: Auguste Renoir, Girl with a Cat (Washington, National Gallery of Art).

shows take place annually in the United States alone. Cat societies enroll as many as 150,000 professional cat breeders, not to mention millions of cat fanciers.

What is it about this animal that has so fascinated humans and endeared itself to the hearts of so many? Perhaps it is the thrill of being loved by an animal that seems fiercely devoted to independence. Perhaps it is the mysterious contradictions cats seem to embody—being both cunning and fierce, yet gentle and tame. The piercing cry of a cat sounds somewhat like a child in the dark, and its purr inspires calm and peace.

Whatever the case, people in numerous ancient settings looked to cats, both great and small, as important symbols, harbingers, helpmates, and housemates. The purpose of this book is to explore cats in all of these settings, from their role in our human world to their participation in some of the world's greatest legends and as living embodiments of the supernatural world.

Although this exploration centers mostly on the domestic cat, great cats wander in and out of these pages too. From leopards, cheetahs, lynxes, and ocelots to the king of the jungle, great cats are our pets' relatives, therefore, the beliefs and stories surrounding house cats cannot be separated from those about large cats.

Likewise, this book reviews the mythical part-cat chimeras and griffins and the symbolic cats that appear in carvings, paintings, coats of arms, and even modern logos. This study reveals much about cats as an important archetype in human awareness—one that even those who disdain cats cannot avoid.

Finally, for those ardent feline lovers whose cats own *them*, this book includes a chapter on choosing and caring for your cat in natural, earth-friendly ways. I count myself among this group, having owned upward of seven cats at a time, most of which joined my family on their own. During the process of adoption, my human family learned much about feline personalities and needs that other cat people should find useful.

Whether or not you own a cat or are simply interested in this purr-snickety animal, these pages embody a fun, frolicsome, feline tour de force that informs, be-mewses, studies, and reflects on the world from a cat's-eye view. You may never look at cats the same way again.

Even the smallest feline is a work of art.
LEONARDO DA VINCI

ONE

THE CAT-A-LOGUE

So, Tiberius might have sat . . . had Tiberius been a cat!
MATTHEW ARNOLD

According to a story from the Middle Ages, the devil invented cats quite by accident. It happened while he was trying to escape God's wrath. In his hurry, Satan tried to create a human, but the result was an animal without skin. When Saint Peter saw this, he pitied the creature and gave it a fur coat from off his back, which became the cat's most valuable asset.

    This story is charming, but the truth is just as intriguing.

THE HISTORY OF DOMESTIC CATS

Our modern cat descended from the Ur-cat of the Miocene *(Pseudaelurus),* which was a lynxlike hunter that lived in forests eating whatever meat it could catch. Ten million years ago, in South America, ocelots and other small cats branched off from this root. Around the same time, in Europe and North Africa the wildcats appeared *(Felis silvestris, Felis silvestris libyca).* The African wildcats eventually developed into the common domestic species known as *Felis silvestris catus.* The Asian wildcats became more the elegant and

*Howard Carter,
mural in Egyptian tomb.*

plush breeds such as the Siamese, Burmese, and Himalayan.

Domestication altered cats very little from their early ancestors. The teeth, cheek muscles, and digestive systems of domestic cats are still those of a meat-eating hunter. The main changes came with increased reproductive capacity and variations in size, fur length, and colors.

Documentable history mentions domesticated cats living in Egypt 3,500 years ago, and other evidence suggests domestication could have begun as much as 8,000 years ago. Among the Egyptians, cats were venerated, being valued for their capacity to protect grain storehouses and deter disease by capturing rodents and snakes. In this region, killing a cat was a serious crime, punishable by death.

To comprehend the depth of the Egyptian reverence toward this creature, one need only look to Persian history around 2,500 years ago. A leader among the Persians, knowing the Egyptian religion and laws regarding cats, instructed his troops to go to war with live cats strapped to their shields. The Egyptian army feared harming any of the sacred creatures, so the Persian forces were able to advance easily. Yet, in an odd inconsistency regarding larger cats, Egyptian priests readily wore lion, tiger, panther, and leopard skins when performing their duties.

A limestone carving found in Thebes, dating to approximately 1900 B.C.E., includes the image of a cat sitting dutifully at the feet of its human family. If the name Bouhaki, which is carved in the stone, belongs to the cat, then this cat is the first cat we know of to be given a name. Alas, Egyptologists have argued over this illustration for years, believing the name actually belongs to a dog also pictured. If so, the honor of being the first named cat then falls to another Egyptian, in the 1400s B.C.E., Nedjem, whose name means "sweet."

Egyptian cat statue (New York, Metropolitan Museum of Art).

From 1300 B.C.E. to 1000 B.C.E. Egyptians used cats as hunting companions for catching fish and birds. The Egyptian word for cat was *mau*, likely based on the sound cats make. In a neat linguistic twist, *mau* also means "light" in Egyptian, alluding to the cat's connection to the sun god Ra (see chapter 3).

The name for cat in Sanskrit is *margaras*, meaning "hunter." The Hindu word for cat, save for diacritical marks, is exactly the same and means "cleanser." Our modern term for cat likely originated with the Aryan *ghad*, from which the Latin *cattus*, French *chat*, Italian *gatto*, German *katze*, and Arabic *kittah* could also feasibly derive. Alternatively, the word *cat* may have originated with the Greek word *catus*, meaning "acute," alluding to the way a cat's eye seems to pierce the darkness.

Phoenician merchants transported Egyptian domesticated cats to Europe around 900 B.C.E. as exotic goods. These cats mated with the wildcat of Europe and created the foundation for domestic cats in that region. In their new homes cats functioned similarly to their Egyptian counterparts, becoming farmhands and city janitors, helping keep rodent and snake populations under control.

Respect for cats waned during the medieval period in Europe when superstitious minds readily associated them with evil and witchcraft. Many people were hanged or burned for just owning a "suspect" cat, that is, one thought to be a familiar spirit. Such a cat could become Sabbat transportation for a witch or a temporary body for the witch's spirit (see also chapter 3).

Another low point in feline history in Europe came around the mid-1500s with the invention of a terrible device known as the cat organ. This musical instrument was popular in Brussels during Philip II's reign. It consisted of a device that held

some twenty cats entrapped, their tails being pulled by a mechanism that made the cats meow in pain. This instrument remained popular for a hundred years! As a counterpoint to this, the very first cat show took place in England in the late 1500s; it included mousing competitions.

Fortunately some felines escaped the witch-hunts, cat organs, cat races, and other tortures by making their way to America with the colonists in the 1700s, being important shipmates. Cats caught disease-bearing mice that endangered the sailors. Since that time the cat remained a favorite human pet, with numerous organizations dedicated to its welfare and protection.

A unique cat charity was established in Amsterdam in 1969. A large barge, called *De Poezenboot,* permanently anchored in the Singel Canal, houses stray cats. This sanctuary is a popular tourist attraction. It expanded to a second barge in 1971, and a third barge may be necessary due to Amsterdam's huge total cat population, numbering well over 50,000. The operation is run completely by volunteers.

Today there are 25 recognized cat species among the "show cats" and dozens more that are not considered in this category. Some cats even have found their way into world records. For example, the largest domestic cat weighed in at 45 pounds, the longest-lived cat reached the ripe old age of 36, the largest litter consisted of 19 kittens, and the most kittens born to one cat in a lifetime is 420!

CAT CHRONICLES

Felines participated in human culture in ways one might not expect. For example, the popular expression "It's raining cats and dogs" originated in the seventeenth century when cats hunted on rooftops in London. Certain adventurous dogs found their way up to follow the cats, and sometimes the animals were caught in rainstorms. This caused them to be washed off the rooftops to the ground near unsuspecting, and quite surprised, passersby.

Another illustration comes in the way people named regions, towns, and cities. An ancient name for Cornwall was Lyonesse, meaning "country of the she-lion." Similarly, Singapore means "lion's city" and purportedly was built on the site where a three-colored lion (symbolic of the triple goddess) was seen.

Here are some other interesting feline anecdotes, showing how cats of many shapes and sizes have left their paw prints on the world's great civilizations and on people from all walks of life:

- One of the world's wonders, the Sphinx in Egypt, combined the image of the pharaoh with that of a lion to illustrate the pharaoh's strength and link to the sun god Ra. In this region and many other civilizations, lions also appeared artistically on doors and gateways as guardians because of the belief that lions sleep with their eyes open. This bit of lore led to lions symbolizing vigilance.

- Hywell the Good (936 C.E.) in Wales created laws that regulated what price could be collected for the sale of cats. He also created laws protecting the animal, including stiff penalties to those caught stealing cats.
- Coats of arms in the Middle Ages regularly featured cats as symbols for organizations, regions, individuals, clans, or families, including King Richard I (also called Richard the Lion Hearted), the royal crest of Scotland (lion), the University of Madras (leopard), the badge of King Henry VI of England (panther), the House of Kay and the city of London (griffin), and the poet John Keats (cat).
- The popular children's rhyme "Hey Diddle Diddle the Cat and

"The Cat and the Fiddle"
(Mother Goose).

the Fiddle" owes its words to Egyptian mythology. The cow is Nut, the great lunar Mother, Bast is the cat, the dog symbolizes Anubis, the fiddle represents Isis's sistrum, and the dish and the spoon are ritual tools.

- Saint Ives, the patron of lawyers, is portrayed with a cat. This image has come to symbolize fairness in justice.
- The flag of Persia features a sun rising over a lion, representing the power of rulership.
- A group of Italian scholars founded the Academy of Lynxes in the early 1600s. The members of this group, including Galileo, dedicated their efforts to debunking superstition and revealing truth, even as the lynx can see any falsehood (see later this chapter).
- In China an emperor's cat received special honors normally reserved for great humans. On its death in the 1500s, a cat named Ch'iu-lung Chung was buried with a gravestone that read, "Grave of a Dragon with two Horns." The Chinese revere dragons as a symbol of longevity and wisdom.
- Winston Churchill's cat helped the war effort in the 1940s by, according to Churchill, acting as a hot-water bottle, thereby saving fuel.
- In the 1950s the Belgian city of Ypres began reenacting an ancient cat carnival called Kattestoet every three years in May. The original festival was cruel, with cats being thrown to their deaths as servants of evil. The modern festival, however, celebrates cats and is attended by thousands of ardent feline lovers. The Kattestoet parade includes historically themed floats of the cat in Egypt, cat proverbs, and witch cats, just to name a few.

- Numerous well-known people throughout history have either loved, feared, or hated cats. Among the cat lovers we find Lord Byron, Ernest Hemingway, Victor Hugo, Leonardo da Vinci, King Edward VII of England, Pope Leo XII, Queen Victoria, Chopin, Darwin, Einstein, Loretta Swit, and Anthony Hopkins. Ailurophobic people (those who fear cats) include Alexander the Great, Caesar, and Napoleon. Cat haters include Pope Innocent VII, Shakespeare, Brahms, and Eisenhower.

(CORBIS/BUDDY MAYS)

Cats at the Hemingway house.

- Looking to modern times, a 500-acre family theme park is scheduled to open in 1999 at the Indianapolis airport dedicated to none other than Garfield, the cartoon cat.

CREATURES GREAT AND SMALL: CATS IN SYMBOLISM

Throughout their history, cats inspired awe, respect, and curiosity in humans. Consequently, cats became important religious and social symbols in natural, supernatural, and fantastic form.

Should you experience times when any of these felines show

up regularly in conversation, dreams, books, TV, or any other venues, consider their symbolism as it pertains to your life presently. The cat may be carrying a message to you or may be revealing itself as a totem animal (see also chapter 4).

Also consider using these symbols for personal development or when you have specific needs. For example, when trying to locate something you cherish, call on the spirit of the griffin for aid. Or, to dispel misrepresentations, invoke the chimera, which rules all miragelike things. Ask the cheetah to aid you with motivation and completing projects, or the lynx to provide insight into perplexing situations.

Here are some historical cat symbols:

Akeru: In Egyptian myth this two-headed lion guarded the gates of sunrise and sunset. This image is related to notions of understanding and integrating the past while looking to the future (see also chapter 2).

Ant-lion: This poor creature was doomed to death at its birth, the lion part being a flesheater and the ant unable to digest meat. Although the concept of such a beast may have originated in a mistranslation, the creature came to symbolize impossible situations, unproductive unions, or a person who serves two masters, thereby failing both.

Baku: A Japanese mythical creature with tiger's feet, a horse's body, and the face of a lion, Baku can be invoked to consume bad dreams and bring good fortune by saying, "Devour, O Baku!"

Bicorn: A creature from bestiaries that resembles a panther, the bicorn feeds on hen-pecked husbands and always bears a Cheshire cat–like grin from having too many husbands to consume! When this creature comes to you, consider if you have been dominating a person or situation for the wrong reasons.

Bjara: A Finnish cat spirit that steals milk, honey, and cream from the home of those it visits, Bjara is akin to a fairy cat and more mischievous than evil.

Bobcat: The bobcat guards secret or hidden matters, living happily alone in rocky cliffs. This creature teaches us how to be alone and use that time for self-development. It also represents the importance of trust and keeping confidences.

Chimera: This fire-breathing lion-horse is said to live in the mountains of Lycia in Asia Minor. Although it is normally considered a Greek monster, some feminist historians believe it is a goddess that was demonized. Thus the chimera can potentially represent the power to overcome injustice or unfair prejudice. Additionally, in Greek tradition the chimera symbolized swiftness, power, stormy winds, and oncoming danger.

Cheetah: The cheetah gets its species name, *Acinonyx,* from two Greek words that mean "thorn claw," referring to this feline's two visible, unsheathed claws. The common name comes from Sanskrit *chitraka,* meaning "spotted one."

The Egyptians, Persians, and Assyrians trained this cat for hunting because of its running speed, which can reach 70 miles per hour. Louis XI of France used trained cheetahs similarly. As time wore on, speed and agility became the cheetah's symbolic correspondence. With this in mind, one might use the image of a cheetah as a component in magic that requires quick, timely responses.

Cheetahs additionally appeared in celebrations that honored Dionysus. In Africa the cheetah is an important totem (see also chapter 3) that receives honor through ritual mimicry.

Cougar: The cougar represents the ability to catch opportunity when it comes your way. There is also an intimation of protecting yourself when necessary and asserting personal beliefs effectively.

Domestic cat: In Egypt, images of a cat slaughtering a serpent represent a victory of law and goodness over chaos and darkness. This would make an excellent image on charms and talismans for protection. In some medieval bestiaries the cat is logically called "mouser," because it catches mice. Throughout Europe, cat images appeared on business signs, including those for inns and taverns. This custom was most popular from the late 1600s until 1750.

Fudog: In China, these half-lion, half-dog images guard against evil spirits, especially those that try to enter homes. They also defend Buddhist law and represent balance. Replicas of Fudogs can sometimes be found in lawn and garden shops and still make excellent guardians of hearth and home. Carry small images of the Fudog when you need more symmetry in your life.

Griffin: The griffin is half lion, half eagle. The thirteenth-century German philosopher and thelogian Albertus Magnus tells us that emeralds were originally discovered in a griffin's nest. The mythology of the griffin originated in Iran but found a foothold in Greece. Greek art shows the griffin pulling the sun's chariot (or that of Zeus) across the sky. Apollo has the griffin as a sacred beast too, making this an excellent all-around solar emblem. The only instance in Greek and Roman tradition in which the griffin is not related to the sun is when it serves Nemesis, the goddess of retribution, whose griffin is wholly black.

Christianity made the griffin an emblem for Saint Mark. According to medieval legend, two griffins spread their wings to receive light and then fly across the sky until sunset, again alluding to the solar aspect of this creature. The griffin's strength was phenomenal according to all accounts. It could carry the weight of an elephant. Thus, an alternative interpretation of the griffin's symbolic value is that of might.

Indian myths refer to the griffin as a guardian of great treasure, calling it a "golden bird." In Eastern traditions the griffin represents enlightenment and sagacity, much like the dragon. When fashioned into drinking cups, griffin's claws were said to warn the owner of poisoned beverages, and one of its feathers dipped in wine could cure any ill. On medieval coats of arms it symbolized tenacity and heroic strength.

Hsien: In China a supernatural lion that sometimes took human form to fight wars, the hsien, when captured and ordered to return to lion form, became the Buddha's mount. This creature represents honorable service.

Jaguar: One of the largest cats, the jaguar represents fertility and power to South Americans. Killing one of these creatures was once part of the rites of manhood. Some shamanic traditions invoke the jaguar spirit to help cure swellings that result from food poisoning, specifically from venison. Others use the jaguar as a kind of familiar into which the shaman can shape-shift.

As with many creatures of power, the jaguar has a darker aspect. For example, South Americans feature the jaguar in stories that correlate to those of werewolves in the European tradition, and in the Amazon people believe sorcerers assume a jaguar form to attack enemies. The roar of a jaguar brings thunder or the presence of a spirit, a black jaguar may become a demon after death, and some tribes believe that a great jaguar will end the world when it eats the sun and moon.

Leogryph: A merged animal formed from a lion and a griffin, the leogryph represents the power of illusion. When this creature appears to you, things are likely not what they seem.

Leopard: Medicine men carried the image of a leopard to enhance magical powers. In Arabia people sometimes named their children after this cat to endow the child with boldness, bravery, and refinement. The Old Testament portrays the leop-

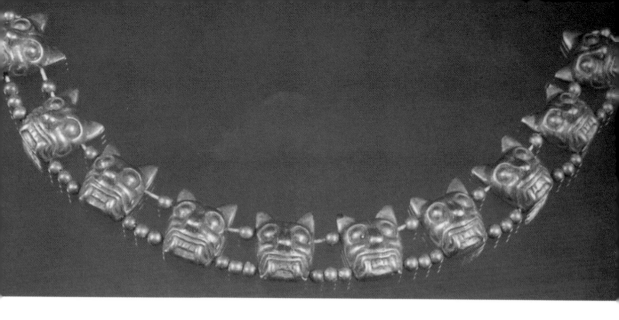

Mayan jaguar necklace (Guatemala).

ard as a symbol of swiftness, shrewdness, and endurance. The Egyptians and Greeks associated the cat with Osiris and Dionysus, respectively.

The Chinese consider the leopard a symbol of ferocity. In Africa it remains an important part of religious observances, where it can represent the storm god or safety from danger. In medieval European heraldry the leopard became the symbol of noble undertakings.

A popular aphorism asks, "Can the leopard change its spots?" When leopards come into your life, consider whether you are trying to make changes for the wrong reason or holding on too tightly to old ways. Alternatively, see if you need to be more protective of something you hold dear; the leopard grants the courage for this along with a warrior's spirit.

Lion: Generally lions are solar symbols, due to their color and their mane, which looks like a sun in splendor. Mithraic tradition exhibits a lion's head with a mane of rays as a solar symbol, and one degree in Mithraic initiation rites was called Lion. In alchemy a red lion represents sulfur and the masculine principle in all things.

In Greek myths lions accompany divine figures (see chapter 3). A twelfth-century treatise on beasts describes the lion as never getting angry unless wounded and never overeating. The writing then counsels that humans could learn much from these traits. During the years of 31 B.C.E.–14 C.E., a lion lying with a lamb symbolized the return to peace and innocence.

In Western culture Christ is called the Lion of Judah, and in the East, Buddha is sometimes seated on a lion throne. Among Buddhists the lion is also a representation of nobility, reliability, sagacity, spiritual energy, and fortune. During Chinese New Year lion dancers perform in front of homes to bring luck and collect money, which is later given to temples for worthy causes.

Africans believe that lions can bear the souls of departed ancestors. The animal is also honored as a familiar and guide, to the extent that some tribes designate the lion with the fond and respectful term of "brother" or simply "sir." Curiously, both African and Tibetan folktales show this powerful creature being outwitted by far less impressive creatures, such as hares (see also chapter 2).

The Assyrians used lion figures to protect their homes, burying them in the foundations or embedding them in walls. In jewelry of this region, the lion represented strength. Among the Babylonians, the lion of Ishtar was symbolic of the eastern quarter of creation and thus of hope and new beginnings. Egyptians often showed a lion as an emblem of summer. This season was also when the zodiacal sign of Leo was most dominant in the Egyptian sky.

Lioness: Female felines, especially the great cats, have strong associations with the Goddess in her Mother aspect. Ancient Greeks used a lioness to honor Artemis, for example.

Lybbarde: A heraldic beast that is half panther and half lion, the lybbarde represents untamed nature.

Lynx: The lynx represents good vision, the ability to discern truth, and clairvoyance, especially in Greece, where myths say that the lynx can see through solid objects. In medieval European heraldry, the lynx also represents wary tenacity and the ability to profit from foresight and vigilance. In Native American traditions, the lynx embodies occult mysteries, about which it remains silent.

Manticore: First described by the Greek physician Ctesias, the manticore is an allegorical part-lion creature with three rows of teeth, a human head, and a tail with spikes. The manticore captures its prey using a hypnotic gaze and poison darts from its tail. Some historians believe the *real* manticore may have

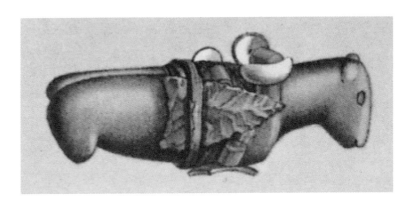

Zuni hunting fetish: mountain lion.

actually been a human-eating tiger. Although a threat to humans, this creature was respected for its powerful jumping abilities, ferocity, and swiftness.

Mountain lion or puma: The Zunis depict the mountain lion as the guardian of the north and the embodiment of power and dexterity, as well as of the fragile balance between the two. In Peru this feline constitutes the constellation Leo the Lion in the night sky, being seen as pouncing on its prey. In many shamanic traditions it has similar connotations to the jaguar as a courier to the spirit world.

Ocelot: A Peruvian cult animal, the ocelot shares many attributes with the otter, such as playfulness and feminine energies.

Panther: Panthers have divergent symbolism. Aristotle and Pliny wrote of the panther as representing treachery, yet in Christian mythology the panther's coat is multicolored and beautiful like that of Joseph. The black panther has associations with the underworld and often bears messages about death in literal or figurative terms.

Some bestiaries report the panther has a sweet but deadly breath, thus giving it the additional symbolic value of insincere communication.

Sea lion: A creature sometimes shown with the upper body of a lion, and the tail of a fish, the sea lion symbolizes courageous actions at sea. Some people believe this creature is partial to children, often saving them from drowning. When one appears to you, it could signal a sea voyage or the need to get yourself out of figuratively deep water.

Serra or saw fish: In the *Bestiary of Philip de Thaun,* the serra bears the head of a lion and tail of a fish. It flies above ships and disables the sails by blocking the wind. The interpretation of this action in medieval bestiaries is that of the devil hindering sacred inspiration.

Sphinx: The Greek sphinx had the head of a woman on the body of a lion. In this form it lay across the road to Thebes, not allowing anyone to pass who could not answer its riddle. Those who answered incorrectly got tossed over the cliff nearby. The person who answered the riddle correctly became a king but

Sphinx (Thames embankment, London).

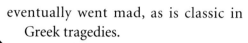

eventually went mad, as is classic in Greek tragedies.

The riddle of the sphinx asks, what walks on four feet in the morning, two feet at noon, and three in the evening? The answer is humankind, which crawls, then walks upright, then walks with the aid of a cane. The sphinx came to symbolize difficult questions that require introspection and wisdom to answer.

Tiger: Western civilization depicts tigers as representing leadership and power, often of a destructive nature. Conversely, in China the tiger is a masculine emblem for courage and authority, with the limitation of sometimes overlooking intuition, which is feminine. This may be why a Chinese version of the story of Red Ridinghood has a tiger as the antagonist. The Chinese also use a white tiger as an emblem of the western corner of creation.

Buddhists use the tiger as a symbol of anger. In Asia people portray the tiger as a shape-shifter, and in Sumatra it is widely believed that human souls can exist in the body of a tiger, having transmigrated there upon death. The people in this region so revere the tiger that they carefully capture a cat before a hunting execution and ask forgiveness for having to kill it.

The Japanese consider the tiger a creature of heroic energy. In Greek art a tiger sometimes draws Dionysus's chariot instead

Opposite: Kali, Nepal

of a leopard. European heraldry uses tigers to denote fierce strength and ruthlessness. In the *Royal Bestiary* on display at the British Museum, illustrations depict the tiger relentlessly pursuing huntsmen who steal cubs, alluding to strong maternal and protective instincts. Finally, because the tiger is one of the few cats that takes to swimming, it has some correlations with lunar energies and the element of water.

As an interesting aside, the word *tiger* may have originated with the Greek word *tygris,* meaning "arrow," alluding to the creature's great speed and balance.

Too jou shen: A stylized creature found in the Ming tombs of China bearing the head and body of a lion, cloven hooves, and a blunt horn, the too jou shen is linked to the unicorn. In Chinese tradition the appearance of a unicorn indicated an honorable, virtuous ruler coming to power.

Uridimmu: A Middle Eastern lion-man whose visage is fiercely protective, like that of a guardian warrior, the uridimmu usually comes to safeguard those to whom it appears from imminent dangers.

Assyrian lion.

What wouldst thou have with me?
Good king of cats, nothing but one
of your nine lives.
SHAKESPEARE, *ROMEO AND JULIET*

TWO
CAT-O'-NINE-TALES

What a monstrous tail our cat has got!
HENRY CAREY

By definition, folklore embraces communal ideas about life and its numerous mundane, ethical, or spiritual questions. Most folklore began as moralistic stories, passed down through familial or cultural lines by oral tradition. In the literally thousands of folktales and their

variations, the symbolic value of cats for teaching and illustrating important lessons was not overlooked.

For example, one of the best known, and most beloved folktale motifs asks the age-old question, "Who will bell the cat?" The fable, which tells of mice trying to figure out how to protect themselves from feline wiles, appears in Finnish, Italian, and North American lore. In other cultural stories, this very same question appears as part of quests. In all settings, the belling of the cat is synonymous with risking one's life for a greater good.

A second fable, called "The White Cat," tells of a beautiful cat who meets a young prince. The prince grows to love the cat with all his heart and asks if she has any wishes. Her request is to have her head and tail cut off and burned. Saddened terribly, the prince grants his beloved pet's request, only to discover something miraculous. It was not a cat at all, but a maiden trapped in the body of a white cat. His unselfish act freed the girl from her curse and united the two in the bonds of true love.

These are but two examples of the many wonderful cat allegories kept alive by diligent bards. This chapter explores several more and also the myths and legends that brought cats to story-time gatherings around the world.

Opposite: Maxfield Parrish,
Puss 'n Boots
(private collection).

THE FOLKLORE CAT

An old Irish folktale recounts the life of a cat the size of a huge cow that ruled over all other cats. Its name was Irusan, and it lived in a cave in Meath. This tale is filled with satire, as when the mice get their whiskers into the cat's egg by way of revenge. Robert Graves theorizes that this story was generated by an oracular cat cult in Ireland. His theory is partially supported by archaeological findings near Meath of a carved silver chair with a black cat sitting in state. Whatever the origins of this story, regional variations provide lessons about not underestimating one's enemy or boasting about ill deeds.

In one story in Ireland and England, a catskin cloak allows a young woman to escape a terrible homelife. This story bears resemblance to "Cinderella" in that the girl, who uses the magical guise of the cloak to escape, meets a prince at a ball and falls in love. The prince gives her a token that allows him to find her, thereby producing the "happily ever after" ending. The appearance of this story in numerous cultures (with minor variations) evidences an underlying human belief that good prevails.

Another folktale motif is that of the helpful animal, aptly portrayed in "Puss in Boots." This story begins with a cat being the only inheritance for a poor child. But it is not an ordinary cat; it is magical. By using its powers, the cat convinces a king that its young master is actually a deposed prince. The cat also helps its master gain the favor of a princess and accumulate

Opposite: Gustave Dore, Puss 'n Boots.

riches. Finally, the cat asks his master to cut off its head, which removes the curse placed on a true prince, who can then enjoy a life befitting him. The moral of this story seems twofold, centering on the rewards for kindness and showing that ingenuity enables one to make the best of a bad situation.

Next we come to the folktale theme of the cat's only trick. In this story a fox boasts mightily about how, if caught in a difficult situation, he had more than a hundred ways to save himself.

The cat, with humility, admitted to having only one—climbing. Yet when a pack of hounds pursued the two, it was the fox that was caught. The cat escaped neatly up a tree. The lesson here is simple: Even "small" talents can be very powerful when used correctly and with modesty.

The great cats also appear in folk stories. Arabic tales began the bardic tradition of a lion capturing a person, then generously letting him or her go free. This story had such appeal that it spread to Europe, where the characteristic of benevolence in lions nearly became a historical "fact." Aesop seems to be one of the few writers to escape this overromanticism, portraying lions as greedy and ravenous.

In Ghana, a folktale tells us why a leopard can only catch prey on its left side. This happens because a leopard asked a domestic cat to teach it to hunt. The cat taught the leopard how to hide when stalking, how to remain quiet, and how to catch food with the left paw. It then told the leopard to practice its art. This the leopard did, but when it got very hungry it resorted to eating the cat's kittens. In anger, the cat refused to teach the leopard how to capture prey on the right side. The moral of the story is that one should never overlook the kindness of others or take it for granted, even when life becomes difficult.

Returning to the beloved house cat, a similar explanative motif occurs. The theme here is the question "Why?" Why do dogs chase cats and cats chase mice? Why do cats land on their feet when they fall?

In answer to the first question, Yiddish lore recounts a time

Lion from medieval astrological manuscript.

Incan sculpture of man and jaguar.

when dogs besought the king to make a law stating humans could not bother canines. When the decree was finally granted, the dogs could not find a place to keep the document safe, so they asked the cats to hide it. A dogcatcher asked for proof of the decree, so a cat went to fetch it, only to discover the paper had been eaten by rats. In fury the cat chased the rats, and the dogs chased the cats, as they have done ever since!

To the question of why cats land on their feet, Native Americans respond that it is all thanks to a human. One day a hero by the name of Manabozo chased a snake away from an unsuspecting cat. The snake was quite angry with Manabozo's interfering with its supper and sought to kill him while he slept. Above Manabozo the rescued cat watched as the snake crept ever closer, and despite the cat's fear it jumped on the snake to keep Manabozo safe. In thanks for the cat's noble efforts, Manabozo declared that cats would always have good eyes and ears and the ability to leap where they wished without ever falling.

Muslim folklore approaches this question a little differently: The prophet Muhammad found his favorite cat sleeping on the sleeve of his robe just when he was called to pray. He did not wish to wake the cat, so Muhammad cut off the sleeve, took the rest of the robe without disturbing the cat, and attended to his religious duties. The cat was so thankful for this gesture that it bowed to him. Muhammad appreciated the cat's courtesy too and in return gave all cats the gift of always being able to land on their feet. Let us hear it for remembering one's manners!

An odd tidbit from Scottish folklore sought to explain a new specimen of cat that developed from domestic cats and wildcats (the *kellas cat*). Local storytellers are quick to explain that this creature is really Cait Sith, a large fairy cat that is all black but for one white spot on its chest. Besides being a friend to the fey, this cat is a witch in familiar form (see also "Breed Beliefs" later in this chapter).

Last, we come to a clever cat in English folklore. In this story, a mouse sat near its mousehole listening. It heard the meow of a cat and remained safely within. Then it heard a dog barking, followed by a spitting cat and the sound of paws running. Thinking all was well, the mouse came out and was promptly consumed by the waiting cat, which, licking its lips, remarked, "I knew it would be good to learn a second language."

MYTHICAL CATS

Myths and folktales are sometimes difficult to differentiate, each having implausible elements. The main thing that sets a myth apart is that it concerns a creature, person, or item believed to have once existed, but there is no historical evidence to support that claim. By comparison, a folktale is often specifically devised as an exaggeration to illustrate a point.

One classical myth, for example, purports to explain why cats carry their young in their mouths, similar to some folktale motifs. It begins with a faithful servant named Galinthias who was the maid of Alcmena. When Alcmena gave birth to Hercules, Galinthias shortened her birth pains. Juno was terribly angry and jealous over this and turned Galinthias into a cat that would have terrible birth pains when bringing forth young by the mouth.

THE GUARDIAN CATS

One recurring mythic theme is that of great cats as powerful guardians. In Egypt, for example, the supernatural two-headed lion Akeru diligently watches the passage into the underworld and the sun's travels through it each night. Its protective powers were considered so archetypal that thirteenth-century art sometimes showed Akeru hitched to the solar chariot. Akeru looks like a sphinx supporting a sun disk in the center of its body, with a head facing each direction. This leads to Akeru's secondary designation of "the Lion of Yesterday and Today." Thus Akeru became a strong emblem of time.

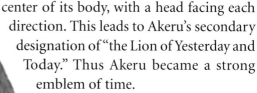

Another set of guardian cats appears in Chinese myths, where five tigers watch over nature. A white tiger rules the western corner of creation, a blue tiger abides in

the east, a black one holds sway in the north, and a red tiger rules the south. The fifth tiger is yellow and unites the other four as caretakers for the earth.

Helping Paws

In Norse tradition, great cats not only protect a goddess, but they also serve her needs. The chariot of the goddess Freya was drawn through the sky by two great cats. Legend says these cats were twins, embodying the attributes of fertility and ferocity. The cats, although huge, were kindly in nature unless provoked.

Similarly providing service, according to Greek and Roman mythology a helpful panther nursed Bacchus/Dionysus as a child. This relationship intimated his tremendous potential for power, but, this godling had to endure numerous trials and tribulations before he could take his place among the gods. Through his story we learn that divine potential lies within all of us, but it takes diligence and endurance to effectively use that power.

Human Cats

An interesting African myth demonstrates the belief that some of the lion's positive attributes can be transferred into humans. The story goes that a long time ago lions sired sons and daughters by human women to whom they taught the art of hunting. The sons could change themselves into lions and often became great leaders who possessed extraordinary strength and courage. The daughters were very beautiful, but quite dangerous, some consuming their husbands when displeased.

CAT INSTIGATORS

Some mythical cycles use cats to explain natural phenomena. For example, in the Amazon the roar of the jaguar causes thunder, and in Incan mythology a powerful jaguar explains the occurrence of eclipses. This creature hungrily attacks the sun or moon. Yet in Brazil the jaguar supposedly gave the gift of fire to humankind. Maybe it was too hot to eat!

Similarly the Dakota Indians say that the moon's waning is caused by mice nibbling away at it until chased off by a celestial cat. Unfortunately this cat sometimes gets overexuberant and eats the moon when trying to catch the mice. This causes an eclipse!

MONSTROUS CATS

A far less pleasant lion-headed creature, the chimera of Greek myth was a terrible monster, which Bellerophon killed with the aid of a lump of lead. The name chimera means "she goat," but it appears as a blend of goat, lion, and

Mexican tiger mask (private collection).

serpent. Interestingly these three animals also correspond to the three divisions of the Hellenic calendar.

A second fearful cat appears in Japanese myths. It is called *kinkwa-neko,* or "golden flowers." Supposedly these reddish-gold cats had the ability to transform themselves into immensely beautiful women. In this form, one can allure unsuspecting human males away from their duties and capsize entire households.

CAT CAMOUFLAGE

In Scandinavian regions there exists the myth of the Butter Cat, which brings gifts of milk, cream, and butter to kindly humans. Known as Para in Finland, and Smieragatto in Lapland, the Butter Cat protects and provides for humans who show compassion to cats. More than likely this myth developed to cover up a good deed by a neighbor who wished not to embarrass a proud but needy friend.

The Butter Cat is not the only instance of a mythic feline devised to hide human undertakings. During the time of the American frontier, travelers often spoke of the Cactus Cat. This was a terrible creature with thorny hair and huge claws with which it tore open cactus for refreshment. For some people this story provided simple amusement by the evening campfire. Others, however, told it in the hopes of scaring off prospectors from a promising gold claim.

Mystery Cats

Myths around the world also discuss mysterious cats, the origins and indeed very existence of which have never been proved or disproved. In Malaysia the natives speak of Harimau Jalor, a huge tiger with stripes that are horizontal instead of vertical. Rwandans have the *ikimizzi*, a cross between a leopard and a lion. The Madagascar cat is purportedly  a descendant of the saber-toothed cats, and for eight centuries African songs have recounted the presence of Mngwa, a ferocious gray cat that attacks by night.

Just when we might think humans have outgrown such stories, we discover the mythical Big Cat of Britain. Reports of this giant cat are noted as recently as the 1980s, similar to those of Big Foot! Most zoologists are quick to discount such tales as exhibits of overzealous imaginations. Even so, people continue to believe Big Cat is a living, carnivorous fossil. Although descriptions range from something like a cheetah to a lynx or lioness, hundreds of sightings have been recorded since the 1960s. One wonders if perhaps the viewers of Big Cat read *Gulliver's Travels* once too often, drawing the Brobdingnagian cat (three times the size of an ox) right from Jonathan Swift's pages!

John William Waterhouse,
The Sorceress.

CATS IN LEGEND

Legends differ from folklore in that they chronicle the lives of important people, events, or organizations, although the stories cannot be wholly authenticated. Generally a legend includes some fantastic element that reveals important characteristics about its protagonist or that teaches a lesson.

A story from Tibet about a noted saint, Milarepa, illustrates legendary traits well. Milarepa was trapped for six months in a cave where he constantly battled demonic forces. When his students finally found him, he had assumed the form of a snow leopard. In this tale, Milarepa is a historical figure. His legendary leopard form becomes a symbol of overcoming great evils within or without—an apt representation for a man who became a saint and a good example to consider in our own struggles against negativity.

One theme in cultural legends is that of the hero overcoming or befriending a lion as a show of strength or compassion, respectively. There is the story of Saint Jerome removing a thorn from a lion's paw and that of Androcles and the lion, both showing the power of goodness. The stories of Daniel in the lion's den and Hercules' defeat of a lion illustrate the power of humankind to overcome seemingly insurmountable odds.

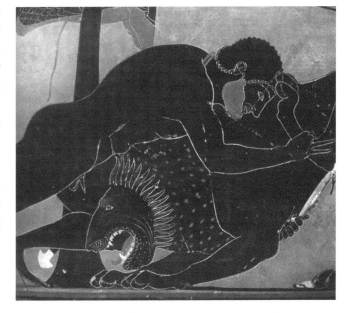

Hercules and the lion, Greek vase.

The story of the chimera also evidences this theme. According to legend, the king of Lycia offered a reward to whomever could slay this monster. Bellerophon came to this king's court with letters of introduction indicating that his sponsor would prefer Bellerophon did not return alive. Thus, this unsuspecting hero was sent to battle the chimera in the hopes that one, the other, or both would die.

Bellerophon proved more cunning than anticipated and enlisted the aid of the winged horse Pegasus by praying to Athena for help. Pegasus was far too quick and agile for the chimera, and Bellerophon slew the beast. After this, Bellerophon and Pegasus accomplished many noble deeds, but eventually the boy became overly confident, trying to ride up Mount Olympus. This attempt met with Jove's thunderbolt, neatly hurtling Bellerophon back down to earth and a more humble attitude.

Many other charming legends include our feline friends. Here is a brief sampling:

Sideshow banner
(Virginia State Fair)

PHOTO BY JON GRAHAM

THE FISHERMAN'S CAT (ENGLAND)

In some rural regions of England, fishermen refuse to cast their nets into the sea before cockcrow and often are seen tossing a few fish back into the water. Legends say that this is all due to a cat. Once there was a girl who was very beautiful but also very spiteful. She cast magic spells to win a lover, who obligingly took her to sea. While out on the boat, the girl whistled up a storm before cockcrow and drowned all aboard, not caring about anyone other than herself. For this act she became a four-eyed cat and forever haunts fishing boats. Thus fishermen give her a bit of seafood to keep the evil away.

The Absentee Cat (Buddhist)

According to some traditions, the cat was the only creature absent from the Buddha's ascension. Before leaving Earth, the Buddha called all the animals, but only twelve answered his invitation. The rat arrived first, being a friendly creature. The ox was second, hating to be late for anything. The tiger sauntered in third, roaring for attention, followed by the timid rabbit and then the dragon, with a regal demeanor that excited everyone. The snake slithered in sixth, captivating all the guests, and the horse arrived seventh, sedately offering aid.

Next came the goat, which hoped to play to the crowd but found itself upstaged by the monkey, who followed just behind. The next celebrant was the rooster, which arrived late specifically to gain attention. The dog walked slowly to the event, arriving eleventh, and the boar came last. In gratitude for these animals' attendance, the Buddha named the Chinese astrological years after them, and said that all people born during those years would bear the named animal's traits.

Unfortunately our feline friend the house cat did not arrive in time for this honor. It stopped to chase a mouse. The intimation here is that "lower" spiritual powers should not participate in the higher workings of the soul.

Master of the Mogul School (State Museums, Berlin).

Strega Cats (Italy)

The cloisters of San Lorenzo house hundreds of cats, but why so many? Local legend claims these cats were once evil wizards intent on defying local law and causing other mischief. Finally the local clergy became irate and the wizards ran off, seeking protection in the cloisters. The priests at the cloisters required a promise from the wizards that they would never again live as witches, but become cats and live at the cloisters in peace. They agreed and have remained there ever since.

Treed Cats (Origin Unknown)

A long time ago there lived a farmer with too many cats. When

Cats from a medieval bestiary.

one mother cat delivered a large litter, he threw the kittens in the river to drown, as he was unable to care for them all. The mother cat begged a nearby willow tree to rescue her young. The willow agreed, taking up the kittens gently. Ever since then small, fuzzy buds appear on the willow branch, left there by the kittens.

An Arthurian Tail (Celtic)

In the region of Lausanne there resided a horrible black cat that slew everything and everyone in its path. When Merlin informed King Arthur of this evil, the king sought to rid the land of it. Merlin helped draw the cat out of its cave near a lake. The fight was bloody, the cat seeming to recoup from even the loss of limbs. Finally Arthur killed the cat by cutting its head from its body and keeping it from returning to the safety of its cave. Because of this great battle the region became known as the Mountain of the Cat. The designation remains today.

Christ's Cat (Christian)

Christ in his travels once came across a starving cat. He gently took the creature into his robes and carried it to the next town, giving it food and water. Here, Christ put the cat into the hands of a follower named Lorenz. When people questioned his actions, Christ used this moment to teach compassion toward all creatures and charge those listening to diligently care for these little "brothers and sisters," much as Saint Francis did hundreds of years later.

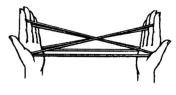

Cat's Cradle (Unknown)

Students of sympathetic magic believe that the children's game of cat's cradle may have been played as a way of capturing the divine sun cat. In areas where it was hot, the cradle gave the sun god a place to rest, symbolically bringing a cool respite. In Arctic areas, the string tangled the cat's feet to keep it in place and retain the warmth.

The Governing Cat (India)

For twenty-five years there were standing orders to the guards at a government house near Poona to make note of, and show arms to, any cat passing in and out of the house. This came about after Sir Robert Grant (governor of Bombay) died in the house in the 1800s. On the night of his death, a cat was seen going out of a door and down a path the governor frequented. A sentry seeing this told others of the governor's transmigration into the cat's body. Thus any cat seen since then is treated with all due honor, just in case!

King of the Beasts (China)

In China a legend tells that cats were the first rulers of the world. After some time of having to handle problems instead of hunt and play, the cats wisely decided the job was not suited to them. They gave it into the hands of humans, the next most evolved creatures. Since then cats have retired to the life of leisure they now enjoy.

BREED BELIEFS

Folklore and legends propose different explanations for how various breeds of cats developed, why they have specific characteristics, how the breeds spread across the world, and what influence cats of various breeds have on their owners. Such stories are a way that our ancestors resolved the mysteries that we now recognize as caused by genetics and odd coincidences that occurred among owners of cats of specific breeds.

For example, there are several stories as to how Angora cats developed such a luxurious coat. One story claims that due to living in the Russian climate a wise cat asked the gods for longer, thicker fur! Similar tales exist about the Bengal cat's spotted coat, one claiming in rather scientific fashion that it developed from the successful mating of a wild leopard in Asia and a domestic feline.

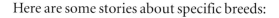

Here are some stories about specific breeds:

AMERICAN SHORTHAIR

Tradition tells us that the American shorthair first came to North America on the *Mayflower* as a pest controller. Whether or not this is true, the shorthair was so valued during the western expansion that cats sold for upward of fifty dollars each!

BIRMAN

Among the many breeds, the Birman has the most mysterious origin. Legends say that a hundred pure white cats with golden eyes guarded the Khmer temple in Lao-Tsun, Burma. This temple was the home of a blue-eyed goddess Tsun-Kyan-Kse, who presided over reincarnation, specifically into the form of a cat for those who were worthy of the honor.

One of these cats was so devoted to its master that it tried to protect him from an invading force. In doing so, the cat had to face the image of Tsun-Kyan-Kse. The goddess saw the cat's devotion and changed its eyes to blue and fur to gold. The legs became brown like the earth, and the paws retained the whiteness of the cat's master's hair. The soul of the master was then reincarnated in his beloved cat's body. From that day forward, the colors of all the temple cats reflect that of the faithful cat (see also chapter 3). For more information on Birmans see page 154 (Cat.com).

Burmese

Common legends have it that Burmese cats were kept in the temples at Burma (see also chapter 3), pampered beyond belief, even having servants! Periodically these cats would be given as a gift to honored guests, which is how they found their way to different parts of the world.

Albrecht Dürer, Saint Jerome

Chartreux

Also called the monastery cat, according to legend the Chartreux cat arrived in France thanks to the monks of the Carthusian order at the monastery of La Grande Chartreuse, near the Italian border. The monks imported the creature from the Cape of Good Hope. Exactly why the monks, famed for Chartreuse liqueur, did this remains unexplained in the legend.

Others say that the Carthusian monks received the cat from knights returning from the crusades. The knights supposedly found the cat in Syria, but no documentation exists to support this or the previous theory.

Japanese Bobtail

Local stories say that the first bobtail arrived in Japan a thousand years ago at the request of Emperor Ichijo, a known cat lover. From that time forward bobtails rightfully became the pets of nobles, who followed the emperor's example.

Japanese woodcuts indicate, however, that the cats may have been in Japan as early as the sixth century, as servants in the Niko and Gotokuji temples.

Korat

In Thailand a Korat brings good fortune to the home. These cats have a silvery blue coat, inspiring people to use them in rain-making rituals, which led to the alternative name "cloud-colored cat." The cat's eyes are compared to young rice shoots, and thus if this cat lives near a rice paddy the crop will prosper. Given to a bride on her wedding day, the Korat ensures abundance.

Maine Coon

By its name alone a cross between a cat and a raccoon is inferred for the Maine coon, no matter how unlikely. Other theories on this cat's origins include it being a descendant of cats belonging to Queen Marie Antoinette of France.

MANX

Legends about the Manx say this creature has the power to see and commune with fairies and elves, being on good terms with both. Thus fairies are said to let the cat in the house if it is put out at night. In Japan similar tailless cats are favored by feline fanciers (*mi-ke* cats, the Japanese bobtail) due to the belief that long-tailed cats can transform themselves into humans and enchant their owners.

Native legend from the Isle of Man tells us that the Manx's tail was lost or gnarled a long time ago when a princess strung rings on her cat's tail. Unfortunately the cat dropped its tail and the rings fell off, so the princess tied them on, forever knotting the tail into a short, bobbed appearance. Another story tells us that the Manx was late arriving at Noah's ark, running in just as the doors slammed shut, neatly reducing the creature's tail.

Other explanations for the Manx's tailless state include the Vikings cutting off cats' tails to decorate their helmets; Samson cutting off a cat's tail to save himself from drowning; and a feudal lord placing a tax on cats' tails, so feline owners in the area simply cut them off!

Norwegian Forest

Cats figure heavily in Norwegian folklore. There was one huge cat in the region, so immense that Thor could not lift it. Two other great cats, owned by Freya, blessed the crops of any farmers who left them gifts of milk in the fields. Whenever the sun shone, people would say that Freya fed the cats well. These legendary cats are sometimes claimed as the Norwegian Forest cat's ancestor.

Ragdoll

A myth of modern origin says that the mother of this breed suffered a pelvic injury while pregnant. Her kittens then came forth abnormally limp and showing little reaction to pain.

Siamese

People in Thailand believe the Siamese with a smudge mark on its back is particularly sacred. It received this mark when a god picked up one of these creatures by the scruff of the neck. Legend also claims this cat got the kink in its tail when it tied a knot in it to remember something. The task was forgotten, but the kink remained.

A favorite legend about the shape of Siamese cats' eyes goes as follows: Two cats were left to guard the goblet of the Buddha for a monk who tended to drink heavily. After a long absence, one of the Siamese went to seek another holy man worthy of safeguarding the artifact while the other kept vigil. The second cat sat so long at this task that her eyes permanently crossed. She finally fell asleep wrapped around the goblet. When her mate returned, he found five kittens, all with kinked tails and squinted eyes!

Another story tells us that the cats got their blue eyes while defending a sacred altar. When invaders came, the cats jumped to aid the monks with a vengeance. In reward, the monks prayed to change the cats' eyes from fiery red to heavenly blue, thereby honoring their service.

TABBY

Linguists believe the tabby got its name from a Turkish word, *utabi*, a striped cloth people wore that bore some resemblance to the tabby's markings. Alternatively it may have been named from the striped, watered silks that originated in El Tabbiana, near Bagdad.

TORTOISESHELL

In Japan owning a tortoiseshell cat is a great boon to sailors. It keeps the spirits of the departed away from the ship and protects the boat from wreckage during storms. Likewise the Celts valued this type of cat, believing it brought positive energy into the home if one came of its own volition (see also chapter 5).

Turkish Van

After Noah's ark came to rest on Mount Ararat and the floods receded, cats began to venture into the city of Van, Turkey. As they walked, God reached down to stroke the cat, leaving its forehead and tail colored brownish red.

Michel-Nicholas-Bernard Lépicié, The Morning Rising *(detail).*

Abuherrira's Cat, * *too here [paradise]*
Purrs round his master blest,
For holy must the beast appear
The prophet hath caress'd.
GOETHE

THREE
SPIRITUAL CATS

For he is of the Tribe of the Tiger.
CHRISTOPHER SMART

The Turkish Van cat was not alone in receiving attention from the gods or acting as a servant to the gods. Cats have appeared in sacred settings around the world.

---

* Abuherrira, a companion of the prophet Muhammad, was known as "the father of the little cat."

Henri Rousseau, The Dream *(detail from painting).*

Some have been honored as tribal spirit guides, others as divine powers, and others still simply as welcome guests in the houses of the gods. Whatever the case, cats hold a place of honor in many religious systems. This chapter examines that reverence.

CAT WORSHIP

Evidence suggests that along with the Egyptians, the Chaldeans, Medes, Persians, and Celts all had some form of cat worship. This reverence continued for thousands of years, but sometimes became its followers' undoing. For example, a Gnostic sect that followed a Persian philosopher and mage named Manes (born 216 C.E.) showed elements of feline reverence. Apparently Manes's teachings contained Egyptian, Buddhist, and Zoroastrian influences, which account for a cat figuring in his followers' worship as an emblem of the sun, moon, and Mithras. Unfortunately Manes came to a bitter end, being crucified around 267 C.E. The subsects of this religion, however, survived for approximately a thousand years, continuing the tradition of cat veneration. One follower, accused of worshiping the devil in the form of a cat, was burned during the reign of Robert I (1027 C.E.).

Two Manichean sects met similarly horrendous ends in Europe in the eleventh century. The authorities claimed that the devil appeared to the followers of these sects as a cat. Pope Innocent III used this gossip to focus a crusade against the Manicheans, resulting in untold numbers of innocent people being slain, burned, and torn asunder along with their cats.

Amazingly, even this savagery did not undo cat worship. As late as the 1700s, cat-centered rituals were annually observed in Province. Here a tomcat was dressed like a child and displayed in a shrine. People threw flowers to the cat and bowed when they passed. Worshipers identified the cat with Horus, who died for his people. Unfortunately the worshipers felt the cat should share Horus's fate. On June 24 (probably because it was the summer solstice) the creature was sacrificed with a bonfire, attended by even bishops singing songs that honored the cat's sacrifice.

Grandville, illustration for Aesop's Fables.

CAT SACRIFICE

To modern minds it is hard to comprehend how and why people would sacrifice such a noble creature, as occurred in the Province festival. In considering these acts,

Kali.

we must understand that the worshipers believed that the sacred animals would have a special place with the gods they represented. Additionally, offering such a valued animal held more weight with the deity being petitioned for aid or blessings.

Generally speaking, the cat was considered a suitable offering for the gods and goddesses of the underworld—the place of mysteries where the sun rested by night. Often a worshiper performed this act when asking for the gift of second sight, something cats supposedly possessed. By sacrificing a cat, its gift could be released into the worshiper. Alternatively, some rather perverse worshipers felt that torturing a creature beloved of the gods would inspire their immediate response so the cat could be released.

Laplanders at least gave their deities time to decide which creature was preferred for sacrifice. A piece of fur from each of several animals, including a cat, was taken to the altar on the ring of a ritual drum. If one of the rings turned toward the image of Thor, the people took it as a sign. Whatever hair was attached to that ring determined which animal became the honored sacrifice while people sang and beat the ritual drum.

Cat sacrifice continued much longer than one might expect, still being noted in the mid-1700s in northern Scotland. Here people used the cry of cats being sacrificed at midnight to overcome a spirit they wished to control. This sound was thought to break a spirit's resistance to the petitioner's orders.

Another example occurred in England in the 1800s. In the region of Albrington people customarily whipped a cat to death at Shrovetide. Cultural experts believe this rite dates back to worship of Apollo, in which the cat represented the moon and was given to the sun to increase its power over the sky.

CLOISTERED CATS

In Babylon cats were welcomed into temples to wander and sit at the side of the gods. People here believed that each cat had a special mission on earth. In fact, some worthy humans could transmigrate into the body of a temple cat upon death, but only if their deeds merited it.

Japanese legend tells us that a cat at Gotokuji temple was responsible for the temple's prosperity. Once the temple had been very poor. Yet the monks shared what little food they had with a beloved pet cat. One stormy day the cat saw a group of wealthy warriors riding toward the temple, so it raised its paw and beckoned them to come in. On account of the weather the warriors had to stay the night, during which time the monks shared Buddhist beliefs with them. One of these warriors eventually returned to study at the temple, bringing with him a sizeable donation. Consequently a small shrine was built to the little cat who made it all possible. This is how the charm

of the Beckoning Cat came to be (see chapter 4).

This story may also explain why Buddhist temples often kept a minimum of two cats at all times—aside from the practical benefit of protecting the temple's manuscripts from mice. The Gotokuji temple remains

Cat pulling a monk on a leash.

dedicated to cats. The altar reliefs still show Maneki-Neki, the Beckoning Cat who brings good fortune and joy. People come here to pray for blessings on the souls of their departed pets.

The Byzantine convent of Saint Nicholas has been a home to cats since the first century C.E. Historians tell us that Saint Helena suggested cats as a remedy to a huge snake population that was continuing to grow due to a long drought. In response to her suggestion her son, the Roman emperor Constantine the Great, appointed Calocaerus to govern the island. Calocaerus imported cats from Egypt, which were then taken to the region now called the Cape of Cats. The monks at the monastery of Saint Nicholas cared for the creatures and the cats kept the snake population under control.

In the 1400s a monk reported that descendants of these first cats still existed in the region. The land suffered terribly from drought and remained desolate, so the cats continued their vigilant service. Likewise in the 1500s a visitor noted that the local monks were obliged to maintain at least one hundred cats for this   work.

This monastery temporarily fell out of use in the late 1500s. Then at some point in time a group of nuns tried to replace the original monks and rebuild Saint Nicholas of the Cats. With the help of the World Society for the Protection of Animals, the cat population was reestablished in healthy fashion, and it remains so to this day.

During the 1300s a brave Muslim warrior by the name of El-Daher-Beybars honored his beloved cats in a unique way. He bequeathed a special garden for them, to be called the Cat's Orchard and placed next to his mosque in Cairo. Here, homeless hungry cats found sanctuary for hundreds of years. Indeed, even after the mosque itself fell into ruin, cats in Cairo often received daily gifts of food to continue this tradition.

In Siam and Burma people continue to believe that cats house the spirits of the departed and therefore welcome them into sacred places. Priests carry purebred Siamese cats into temples in golden cages, burning incense to them and offering them special foods. Cats in this region are also often brought to witness important functions of state, such as a coronation.

In the 1940s it was reported that a rare type of cat, similar to the Siamese but larger and darker, appeared in the temples of Tibet, where they were kept as sacred animals. Another report

surfaced in the 1960s when two of these cats were imported for breeding, but the cats turned out to be Birman cats. The theory goes that when Burmese priests were forced to leave their temples at the turn of the century, some found sanctuary in Tibet, taking their cats with them and thus establishing the breed there.

Saint Patrick was another who bred cats, beginning a tradition that still exists in some Irish monasteries. Many cats have thus become the honored pets of religious sects.

These are but a few examples that demonstrate cats walking

deftly in hallowed halls where even some humans are forbidden to go. An interesting modern offshoot of cloistered cats are those that serve in libraries and post offices. The palace library at Saint Petersburg, for example, once employed more than three hundred Russian cats to keep rats under control. As late as 1987 so many libraries had resident cats that the Library Cat Society was founded in the United States.

Similarly, post office cats have been employed by the British government for over a century. It began in 1868 when some postal money orders were eaten by rats. The post office involved requested three cats be appointed to control the problem. In response, a shilling a week was given to the office as an allowance for the cats. By 1980, 25,000 cats were employed, making a lucrative £2 a week.

CAT NUPTIALS

Some cats abide in temples, and others get married in them. In the 1980s cat unions became a popular idea among feline fanciers, to the extent that a Universal Life minister began performing ceremonies for upward of $300 each. Rumor has it that the marriage cup gets laced with cream and the cake is fashioned from tuna. One wonders if catnip was thrown at the happy couple after the ceremony instead of rice!

CAT CANTICLES

Someone listening to a tomcat's song might not think of music, let alone music suitable for the gods. This did not deter the Egyptians from finding a way to give cats a place in musical history.

One of the most ancient and widely used musical instruments for magic, religion, and ritual is the Egyptian sistrum. Because of its construction, historians believe this rattlelike instrument, dedicated to Hathor, also had strong connections to cat worship. The sistrum features a cat at the pinnacle of an ankh-shaped outer frame. The frame symbolizes life and well-being, and the cat represents fertility, the maternal nature, and lunar energies. Four bars are suspended inside the oval frame, signifying the four elements. These bars create the rattling sound, which symbolizes manifestation and universal harmony. Egyptians used the sistrum to accompany sacred dance and songs. They introduced it to Italy, where the instrument appeared in the worship of Isis during the Roman era.

Interestingly, this is not the only instrument that somehow connected cats with worship of the divine. In Japan a three-string instrument called the samisen was regularly used to accompany singers in religious rituals. Until the early 1900s the samisen was strung with strings of actual catgut. Geishas went so far as to perform regular masses honoring the cats that gave their lives to make the samisen and its sacred music.

Bast with sistrum and kittens.

CAT PARADISE

So strong is the human reverence toward cats that some feline spirits are thought to continue to exist after death. The Egyptians took this concept to a pinnacle by mummifying cats so they could enjoy their afterlife in a fitting form. Additionally, the Egyptians provided cats suitable food for their new existence so they would not hunger on their path back to the gods.

Along its journey a cat spirit received help. A god grasped the cat's paws to keep it headed in the right direction and offered aid if the timid feline faltered. On finally arriving in paradise, a cat was assured of bliss, receiving abundant hunting grounds and fish.

Etruscan art depicts a similar end for cats, showing cats' souls happily dwelling in the otherworld. In one piece in particular, cats are shown participating at a great banquet table with the rulers of the underworld. Analogously, in Malay, cats hold special honors in paradise because they lead the way from hell to heaven, spraying water on the needy along the route.

Goethe wrote about various animals attending their masters in paradise, including a cat resting at the feet of the prophet Muhammad. Indian tradition provides a paradise for cats too. They are welcome in the heaven of Devendiren, where 48 million goddesses dwell.

Egyptian cat mummy (British Museum).

Cat herding geese, from an Egyptian papyrus.

CAT MAWS AND PAWS

After cats leave this world, some seem to be adopted by gods and goddesses, who use cats as servants or forms. Freya in the Norse tradition and Cybele in the Phrygian tradition, for example, both rode in chariots drawn by felines. In India the goddess Shakti rides a cat when going to aid a child or a woman giving birth, and in the Etruscan tradition the goddess Diana sometimes assumes the form of a cat.

As with many animals, early people also depicted cats (in all their forms) as aspects of the divine. By far the best known is Bast, the Egyptian cat-faced goddess. Bast was considered a sun goddess of beneficence, joy, dance, and fertility; she was sometimes depicted as bearing the face of a lion. Oddly, Bast represented the moon too, her golden eyes being the sun god's means of viewing matters on earth by night. Bast also embodied the beneficial traits of the fire element. Another Egyptian goddess, Sekhmet, controlled the fierce, consuming fire of divine wrath.

During April and May a special festival was held in Bast's honor. This took place in Bubastis (the city named after Bast) and was attended by as many as 700,000 people. Bast and her minions were so revered that it was a crime to kill cats in Egypt, punishable by death. Archaeologists have uncovered mummified cats here, their owners apparently wishing for the companionship of their cats even in the afterlife.

Not all cat deities were as kindly or influential as Bast. The Danish goddess Black Annis was a version of Danu thought to be fierce and savage. Art depicts her as having huge teeth and fingernails. Similarly, Cailleach Bheur in Scotland was a terrible cat goddess whose name means "Blue Hag of Winter" and who demanded human sacrifice. Another malevolent figure is that of Ccoa in South America. This god appears with a tail, stripes, glowing eyes, and a stream of hail issuing from his ears, which Ccoa uses, along with lightning, to destroy crops. The only way to satisfy Ccoa is with offerings of magical goods.

Such negative depictions of divine cats had much to do with the power embodied in large cats like the lion, and their association with feminine attributes. By representing cats in this way, myths taught about the dangers in misused power and, in some instances, helped promote the patriarchy. We can be thankful that many other cultures balanced out the negative associations with potent and beneficent divine feline figures. For example, a divine domestic cat appeared in Peru as the god Al apaec. Al apaec was a supreme god characterized as an old man with fangs and cat whiskers or a cat face with human eyes. This deity is kindly toward humans, taking care of farmers, fishermen, hunters, and

Precolumbian puma.

Apollo the sun god; the middle head of the beast at his feet is a lion.

musicians and presiding over matters of health and fertility. Two of his sacred animals, in addition to the cat, are a lizard that serves him and a dog that is his friend.

Much more so than small cats, it was the great cats who ruled the heavens as the popular companions, assistants, and aspects for the world's gods and goddesses. Not surprising, the most frequent mention of felines occurs in the Egyptian pantheon. Here are just a few examples from around the globe, listed with thematic realms to consider in your spiritual pursuits:

Johann Daniel Mylius, engraving (Philosophia reformata).

Agassou (Haitian): The panther god Agassou protects the traditions of the area.

Anat (Canaanite): A goddess of fertility and love, Anat has for her sacred animal a lion.

Apedemak (Sudan): A god with a lion's head, Apedemak presides over matters of war.

Apollo (Greece): Apollo was believed to be the creator of lions, whereas his sister Artemis created domestic cats.

Aradia (Italy): According to tradition, Aradia was conceived when Diana became a cat and seduced Lucifer, her brother.

Bahu (Hindu): The goddess of creation, Bahu was depicted as the constellation of Leo.

Chnouphis (Gnostic): The sun god Chnouphis has a lion's head crowned with twelve rays and the body of a serpent. His image appears on amulets for health and long life.

Freya (Scandinavia): Freya's chariot is drawn by cats, specifically lynxes.

Tantric painting of cat demons.

Getesh (Syrian): A goddess of love, beauty, nature, and health, Getesh is shown in regional art as standing on a lion. Her other symbols include the lotus and the mirror.

Kali (India): The creative-destructive goddess Kali rides a tiger to her tasks, signifying her great power. Kali is not recommended for spiritual applications, as her anger is swift and unforgiving.

Kwan Yin (China): The goddess of fertility and health, Kwan Yin is sometimes depicted with a lion cub in her arms. Kwan Yin teaches about magic and divination.

Lamashtu (Assyro-Babylonian): The leopard goddess Lamashtu is very malevolent, inflicting plagues and other destruction. The only way to avoid these evils is to coax her back to the underworld with tempting gifts such as sparkling jewels. She is not recommended for spiritual pursuits.

Lion Goddess (Palestine): The lion goddess was the consort of Jehovah in the fifth century B.C.E., when the two powers were worshiped together.

Maahes (Egypt): The lion god Maahes is the son of Bast and Ra. Lion cubs were often raised in Maahes' temples. This deity presides over necromantic divination, occult knowledge, and communication with the spirits of the departed.

Mafdet (Egypt): The lynx goddess Mafdet predated Bast as a life giver and protectress.

Mihos (Egypt): The golden lion god Mihos is filled with nobility, passion, and sexual prowess.

Min (Egypt): A god of fertility and sexual prowess, Min was sometimes depicted with a lion's head.

Narasinha (Hindu): The fourth incarnation of Vishnu, Narasinha appeared as a man with a lion's head.

Nergal (Babylon): A god of the hot summer sun, Nergal has for his emblem a lion. He is not recommended for spiritual pursuits as he has a temper to match his fire.

Pakhet (Egypt): The lioness goddess Pakhet's name means "she who scratches." Unlike her name, however, Pakhet is a protective mother, loving and defensive.

Pallas (Greek): An ancient moon goddess in Athens and figurehead of a feline tribe, Pallas was shown riding a lion. This goddess was invoked as the "one mother of god" similar to Mary.

Ptah Seker (Egypt): The creative source, master of darkness and chaos, Ptah Seker is actually a form of Osiris, depicted as a cat who walks the night without leaving a trace.

Qadesh (Phoenician): The consort to the god of the west, Qadesh has a lion attribute.

Renenet (Egypt): The goddess Renenet, who gives children names, characteristics, and fate, was depicted as a lioness-headed woman.

Ruti (Phoenician): The god Ruti's name literally means "he who resembles a lion." Ruti was the god of Byblos.

Sef (Egypt): The god of yesterday, Sef is embodied in a lion. Realms: integrating and coping with the past.

Sekhmet (Egypt): The lion-headed goddess Sekhmet represents the destructive solar fires and defends divine law without sympathy. Images of this goddess appeared on temple doorways as the guard-

Sekhmet

ian of ancient wisdom. She is the patroness to bonesetters.

Seshat (Egypt): The goddess of books and recordkeeping, Seshat wears the mantle of a feline.

Tefnut (Egypt): The lion-headed goddess Tefnut, daughter to Ra, rules over rain and dew with fertile and creative aspects.

Tezcatlipoca (Aztec): Tezcatlipoca, the god of warriors, was often shown as a jaguar.

Yaghuth (Arabia): A god whose name means "he who helps," Yaghuth was worshiped in the image of a lion.

There are several ways to use the knowledge of cat gods and goddesses effectively in magic. First, you may choose to call on a feline deity when performing spells or rituals for your cats or when calling for a familiar (see chapter 3). For example, Renenet might be well suited to a kitten's blessing, whereas Kwan Yin is appropriate when enacting a procedure for your cat's health and well-being.

Second, you may look to these divine figures when you wish to develop or integrate specific cat attributes. When you need courage, stamina, balance, cunning, or the ability to blend into your surroundings, consider which feline best represents that characteristic, then call on a corresponding god or goddess. The only caution in both applications is to know a little of the culture in which the divine being lived, how to honor that presence in your sacred space, and how to pronounce the deity's name correctly.

CAT SPECTERS AND GHOSTS

The souls of cats who do not find their way to the gods may continue to roam the earth as they did in life, even as the spirits of some humans do. In Combourg Castle, for example, a ghostly black cat sometimes appears on a staircase. It comes, apparently, to keep the former count, who died there, company.

In the early 1900s the Society of Psychical Research reported the reappearance of one member's cat in ghost form, walking on the grass or hiding in the hedges. Another report from this era speaks of a ghost cat that did not appear but was content to be heard serenading its earthly owners and lapping up an invisible bowl of cream.

Yet another tale from England recounts the story of a young woman who had taken ill. She wondered why her cat did not visit her as usual but thought the creature might be attending to its sick kitten instead. Finally, toward the end of her illness the cat came into her bedroom, rubbing her mistress and purring, then left. When the young woman remarked about this to a maid, the woman appeared shocked. Apparently the girl's cat had died two days earlier, but no one told her the truth due to her fragile condition.

Such stories indicate two things. First, the psychic nature of the cat endures, at least symbolically if not literally. Second, many people love their cats as much as they would a child. In the moments when the unseen world touches our reality, some of these "children" reappear. Whether this appearance is but a psychic

impression left on the area or whether the cat hopes to console its master, one cannot be certain, because the phenomenon is not confined to domestic cats.

Cat in Pere Lachaise cemetery in Paris.

In Paraguay, for example, people talk of a ghost jaguar. This ghost has grayish-white markings and when seen it disappears without a trace. Some scientists claim that it is actually an albino jaguar. Such explanations for spirit cats are not uncommon. For example, the cries of a ghost jaguar in Waracabra are supposed to actually be the trumpeter bird, and sightings of a ghostly saber-toothed water tiger in South America are explained

Victor Brauner, The Philosopher's Stone.

away as giant otters or crocodiles. As there are no physical remains of the ghostly creatures, we may never know the truth.

What we do know for sure is that the belief in an afterlife for cats and other creatures has enough devotees to have created a whole new paranormal industry—that of animal mediums. Like the psychics who contact the spirits of dear departed humans, these mediums travel the astral realms in search of pets whose presence is sorely missed. How one can tell for sure that the right feline (or any feline, for that matter) has been reached, remains dubious. Perhaps the sense of peace and closure this effort gives to humans is reward enough.

FOUR

BROOMSTICKS AND BLACK CATS

Common superstition in the Middle Ages claimed that an old woman seen speaking with a cat was actually conversing with the devil. Such beliefs led to the burning of hundreds of innocent cats during the witch-hunts. As late as the 1800s, a woman who owned a black cat was thrown into a pit, accused of being a witch. What exactly caused people to think that cats were witch animals?

Several theories exist on this. One comes from a Greek legend about a giant named Typhon. Typhon breathed fire, causing great destruction wherever the flames touched. Typhon used this weapon to try to rule over everything, even the gods. One goddess, Hecate, who presided over magical matters, turned herself into a cat until the danger passed. Thus the cat became a special witch animal.

Certain shamanic traditions indicate that cats such as jaguars may be familiar spirits of magicians. Mexicans saw the jaguar as an embodiment of the forest spirit. Such beliefs, if circulated by oral tradition and through merchants and traders, could have fueled the misrepresentation of cats in popular culture.

Another theory states that the unearthly glow of cats' eyes,

(sometimes referred to as hellfire in medieval manuscripts), their uncanny knack for balance, and their ability to hide caused the correlation. Some historians also note that nature worshipers sometimes attended ritual fires dressed in furs to invoke animal spirits, giving rise to the idea of witches transforming into cats. Whatever the case, cats and magic became firmly associated with one another. Cats, along with frogs, dogs, and birds, were "witch animals," to be feared or welcomed, depending on your viewpoint.

CAT-A-CLYSM: CAT COMPONENTS IN OLD SPELLS

In the old grimoires—collections of spells—several magical spells called for the use of feline parts in rather unsavory ways. In reading the examples that follow, bear in mind that the use of animal parts and blood in magical procedures is a very old custom. Animals were originally used in the belief that the creature could provide the magician with its best attributes (see, for example, the formulas to enhance courage listed below). Blood added power, being the font of life.

Beyond this, early mages sometimes hid true magical procedures beneath the guise of odd phrases or instructions to

Paws from heraldic device (left), tiger skull (right).

protect their art. Additionally, the old grimoires are not always a reliable source of true magical traditions, sometimes being penned by those wishing to dethrone pagan practices through fear and misrepresentation. These two factors working together left little information, other than oral tradition, to help modern researchers sort fact from fallacy. For example, when we read that necromancers used cat blood to inscribe curses on linen, this "blood" may have actually been an herbal preparation, the components of which the wizard wanted to keep a secret. Or this information may have been written to inspire antipathy in an already-superstitious public.

Here are some other spells from the past that include cats or cat parts among their constituents:

- To inspire love, mix apple juice, honey, ginger, and ten apple seeds with a few drops of blood from a black cat and put it in the food of your intended.
- To deter a witch, place blood from a black cat on his or her doorway at midnight.
- To ensure yourself of strength and courage, eat of the heart of a lion that you yourself hunted and killed.
- To ensure devotion mix wine with the brain of a cat, your own blood, and vervain. Cook this mixture, strain, and serve to the intended person.
- To relieve eye pains, take the head of a black cat and burn it to powder. Sprinkle this over the eye daily until the pain disappears.

- To increase strength, grind tiger bone and mix with wine.
- To ease joint pain, lay the skin of a black cat daily on the affected area (nowadays this might equate to allowing a cat to lie on your lap).
- To see what others cannot, anoint your eyes with the fat of an entirely white hen mixed with the bile of a male cat.
- To rid yourself of a cold, sneeze on a cat and then chase it away. This spell is based on the idea of disease transference, used often during the Middle Ages. Healers symbolically "attached" illnesses to trees or animals in the hopes that the object would absorb, or the creature carry, the sickness and leave the patient whole.
- To cure a sty, pluck one hair from a cat's tail on the night of a new moon and rub it against the sty seven times. Burn the hair or throw it in running water moving away from you. Warts can be cured similarly, but use the hair from the tail of a tortoiseshell tomcat.
- To inspire courage, gather a live lion's fur and make a girdle from the hairs. Weave the girdle yourself, by hand, between the hours of midnight and sunrise.
- To develop valor, mix the eye and blood from a black cat with dried snakeskin in wine. Soak an eagle's feather in this mixture for three days. Afterward dab the potion on yourself as needed.
- To cause discord give people wine in which the ear of a black cat has been soaked along with rose thorns and dried ants.
- To internalize wisdom and courage, eat a lion's heart. Or bury

the heart near your home to protect against lightning.

- To see clearly in the dark, anoint your eyes daily with dried, powdered cat's eyes mingled with honey.
- To invoke spirits, mix man's gall with the eyes of a black cat and burn them on the ritual fire.
- To transfer any malady into a cat, place one finger in the creature's ear, then chase the cat away.
- To cure paralysis, eat lion meat (recommended by Albertus Magnus).
- To make yourself invisible, wear the ear of a black cat boiled in milk on your thumb (another recommendation by Albertus Magnus).

We can be thankful that for all animals such practices have gone by the wayside in favor of more earth-friendly approaches.

A FAMILIAR FACE

Another way cats appeared in magical traditions was as familiars—partners, if you will, in a wizard's or witch's workings. According to prevalent tradition, the occultist could send a familiar out on tasks, see through the animal's eyes, and even shape-change into that animal. Perhaps the most popularly acclaimed familiar was a black cat. Unfortunately this led to many cat owners being wrongly accused of witchcraft and many cats being executed along with their masters.

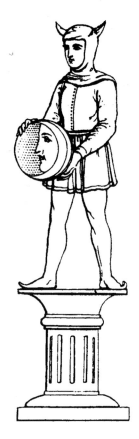

A wizard in a cat-eared costume, calling on the power of the cat.

Witch shape-shifting into cat (16th-century manuscript).

For example, during the fourteenth century in Europe, when the witch-hunts were at a peak, cats were used as evidence of fraternizing with the devil. In the early 1300s the Templars were prosecuted in France for worshiping a magical head and consorting with a cat! Truth be known, King Philip IV was only using these accusations as a way of liberating the Templars' property.

In modern metaphysical traditions people still believe in familiars but define them slightly differently. Familiars are magical partners, trusted friends, and companions— certainly not mere pets. These creatures have a unique rapport with their human counterparts and a deep, abiding kinship that expresses itself in both mundane and spiritual ways. For example, my familiar cat responds to me when I call, eagerly greets me at the door, and rolls around happily in any area where magical energy abides.

Cat familiars provide their human counterparts with insight into people and situations. Frequently a cat will shun a person carrying excess negativity, for example, or one wishing harm to the cat's human companion. Cat familiars help protect the home by watching activities that their owner cannot see and potentially recounting those things through dreams or gestures. For those with children who have "invisible friends," cats often confirm the presence of spirits or fairies by playing with the children's friends too. These services are above and beyond the familiar's aid in magical settings, such as during divination, when the cat might place a paw on a significant tarot card that you overlooked.

How does one come by a cat familiar? That is a difficult question, as many times what we think we need and what the universe provides are two different things. There are ways to call for a familiar, however, using items that cats love as magical helpmates for the rite.

To begin, gather some catnip, a bowl of dry cat food, and a toy mouse and go to your door. Place these items just outside the door and close it. You might wish to request the assistance of a feline deity at this juncture, to better direct your energy (see

chapter 2 for options). Next, close your eyes and visualize your home, your face, and your neighborhood. Extend that vision outward so that a receptive animal can follow the energy to its source. A true familiar does not need (or deserve) coercion to come to you. Keep the vision strong and focused until you somehow sense the message being received.

At this point in the ritual, open your door to symbolically open the path for your familiar. Gather up the items left there, bringing them into the house even as you hope to bring your familiar in. Keep the tokens in a safe place until a familiar makes itself known to you, then give them to the creature (if it is indeed a cat).

Once your familiar feline arrives, you may wish to improve your rapport. Scottish witches sometimes perform a spell with their familiar *mawkin* (cat) to accomplish just that. During this ritual a silver charm is blessed and placed on the cat (as part of its collar), followed by a gift of food and cream. You may wish to adapt this concept, finding an appropriate gift token (such as a name tag with your phone number) for your cat. Bless and energize the token before making the presentation, then spend a goodly amount of time petting and praising your cat so the energy can begin its work.

CAT TOTEMS

In shamanic traditions, people sometimes become aware of an animal guide or totemic spirit that walks with them. In some cases this spirit represents the person's truest nature. Here the totem is a lifelong emblem that one can focus on for development and personal understanding. Take a person who has an ocelot life totem. This individual might need to play to fully release his or her creative abilities but rarely does so. Focusing on his or her totem can help release the inner child and unblock those creative juices.

Leroy Ramon Archuleta, Leopard.

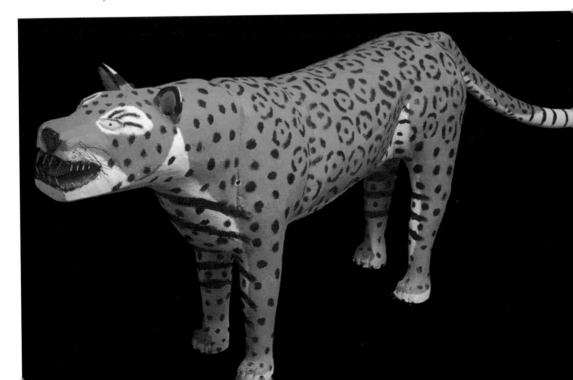

In other instances a totem may appear temporarily to highlight characteristics a person needs to develop. For example, a person with a lion totem might need to learn how to speak up for himself or herself. A person discovering a griffin totem may be receiving a gentle nudge indicating a need to heighten his or her perspectives and see the bigger picture.

If you begin having dreams in which a cat comes to you and teaches you things, if felines begin appearing in odd places and times in your life, or if a cat pops up in the media everywhere you look, you may have a cat totem. Exactly what an individual's totem means is very personal. To more fully understand the significance of a totem cat, consider what type of cat has come to you (see chapter 1), what personal meaning that feline may have for you, and what is happening in your life. For example, if you have been ill and begin dreaming (or seeing images of) a jaguar, this animal has likely come to increase your power to overcome your malady—a sort of spiritual booster. Here are a few other cat totems and their more commonly associated symbolisms:

Bobcat: psychic awareness, true seeing, hermetic retreat

Cougar: testing one's limits, honing skills, self assertion, opportunity knocking

Domestic Cat: self-sufficiency, ingenuity, magical awareness

Leopard: improved instincts, reciprocity with one's environment, personal potential

Lion: group dynamics, parenting skills, tactical protection

Lynx: dexterous movement, revealing secrets, clairvoyance

Panther: aggressiveness, multitasking, territorial nature, pacing oneself, making deadlines, personal quests

Tiger: maternal instincts, mysticism, sensuality, adventure

CAT GENIES

Assyrian incantations addressed elemental beings that we now call djinni or genies. According to this tradition, for every child born, a genie is also born. This creature has awesome powers, including the ability to appear as an animal, such as a cat. In one Egyptian story, a cat genie came to a poor householder begging for food and water. When given a bit of each, the genie rewarded the man with a bit of gold. In certain regions of Egypt it is still considered potentially hazardous to answer the call of a cat at night. It could be a genie, and not all of them are as kindly toward humans as the one in this story.

A story from Japan tells us of such an evil genie, which appeared in the form of a great feline. This cat required human

PER VN BACIO DATO
DA VNA BELLA E GRANDE SIGNORA
AD VN GATTO
SONETTO

Questo, scolpito in tela amabil Gatto,
Gustò di Bella Dea bacio amoroso,
E al Viuo poscia fattone il Ritratto,
Si tien ben custodito, e assai geloso.

Affinchè possa appien serbarsi intatto,
Qual Armellin, che uiue timoroso,
E acciò preso non sia, sen fugge ratto
A stare in Bosco, o in luogo più nascoso,

Cosi Tù ancora, o Gatto auuenturato,
Serba intatta la Bocca, e puro il Core,
E à Colei pensa sol, che ti ha baciato;

E fà che solo a Mè permetti Amore,
Che un Bacio scocchi, e mi riprendi il dato
Bacio Amoroso per temprar l'Ardore

sacrifice, that of a fair woman. On hearing of this, a brave warrior secured the aid of a huge, courageous dog, which took the woman's place in a sacrificial cage. When the spirit cat arrived, it met its defeat on canine teeth and our hero's sword. Since that time, however, the cats who served this spirit and their descendants were doomed to live in exile. Any human who comes across them risks being enchanted.

Opposite: Portrait of Ermine cat with Sonnet (Museo di Roma).

APPLIED CAT MAGIC

Cats have a firm paw in magic, and many people who have cats or cat familiars enjoy making them a regular part of metaphysical procedures. There are numerous ways of doing this, but some precautions should be taken. First, if you plan to welcome your cat into the sacred space, always watch that candles, cauldrons, and cups with liquid are placed where the cat will not upset them. Second, any herbs you work with that might harm the animal should be well out of its reach. Other dangers for cats include snippets of thread, which if consumed can cut through their digestive tract, and athames, ritual knives that can pierce a paw.

Remedios Varo, detail from The Revelation. (2000 ARTISTS RIGHTS SOCIETY (ARS), NEW YORK/ VEGAP, MADRID)

   With these dangers averted, you can welcome your cat into the sacred space without worry. If you are allergic to cats, you can use them in magical procedures symbolically. Samples of magic performed for

or with cats and magic that uses cat emblems as spell or ritual components follow.

Cat Charms, Amulets, and Talismans (for Humans)

Not only live cats but also the images of cats embody magical power. Medieval mages recommended that those born under the sign of Leo the Lion, for example, would do well to wear an onyx stone engraved with the cat to bring luck. A thirteenth-century lapidary recommended carving the image of a lion on garnet to preserve health and protect the bearer from any dangers when traveling; a lion carved on jasper conferred on the wearer the ability to combat poison or fevers. In all these examples the lion as a great cat is a solar symbol indicative of strength and power for overcoming ills. Here are other examples:

- The Egyptians trusted in the power of a living cat to protect them from all ills. If they could not afford to own one, they would instead carry a small carving of a cat blessed with spells or words of power as an amulet. Such carvings can be found today in many nature shops that carry semiprecious stones and crystals.
- Malaysian witches use tiger whiskers and claws as potent charms for strength, luck, love, wealth, and protection. In Ceylon a comparable tradition exists, that of using tiger claws as charms against wild animal attacks. Collecting such items in an earth-friendly manner might be difficult. An alterna-

tive here might be carrying an image of a tiger carved in a red-colored stone (such as carnelian). Such images are also said to ward against disease.

- Lion images carved in jasper protect the wearer against fever; one in garnet is a good amulet for safe travel. During the Middle Ages a charm that bore the image of a great cat could cure kidney trouble or stomach pains. This might translate well into one component for a health amulet. Both lion and tiger images were used frequently on amulets to protect the bearer from the evil eye. Consider this symbolism when trying to turn negativity.

- In Japan the image of a cat with its paw raised, known as *Maneki-Neki*, is considered a charm for improved fortune and prosperity. It is called the Beckoning Cat. Worn or carried, the cat brings luck and health. Images of wood or clay placed in or around a building keep the occupants safe (see also chapter 2).

- In China a cat's image painted on a lantern is used to ward off evil influences. Try carving a cat's face into your magical candles or a pumpkin, or paper-clip a photograph of

A Barong mask from Bali.

your cat to a living-room lamp shade.

- Cats both large and small have the ability to walk in an area without leaving paw prints. If you need to feel less visible in a specific situation, carry the imprint of a cat's paw as an amulet. To make the imprint, gently put a cat's paw into nontoxic ink then press it on parchment. And if you want to put something securely away and keep it well hidden, bind this image to the object to be concealed.

- The Savoy Hotel in London, England, uses the image of a cat carved out of wood for good luck. This cat, known lovingly as Kaspar, takes the fourteenth seat at a table when only thirteen guests are present. One guest to enjoy Kaspar's company was none other than Winston Churchill. If you can find a small three-dimensional cat carving, try carrying it with you

Kittens by a pool, Chinese painting.

to improve your fortune or keep it in your home and use it to bless your meals, as Kaspar would do.

- Carry the image of a tiger when you need more self-control, especially with anything that hinders judgment, or anything addictive. According to superstition, tigers so dislike the scent of alcohol that they will tear apart the drinker.
- In China it is customary to put the image of a cat on the walls of a house during the silkworm breeding season. This image wards against rats destroying the crop. Some farmers even go so far as to assemble live cats to patrol the breeding fields. You might consider using the image of a cat anywhere that guardian energy is needed.

Cat Amulets, Charms, and Talismans (for Cats)

- Place elder flowers in any areas where your cat plays or sleeps regularly. According to folklore these act as a protective amulet, keeping the animal from any maladies.
- Take a small silver bell and bless it with protective energy. Attach this to your cat's collar so that each time the bell rings it sends out positive energy for your feline friend's well-being.
- Mix up a batch of valerian and catnip, and place equal amounts in red (fire), yellow or white (air), blue or purple (water), and black or brown (earth) sachets. Sew these tightly shut. Next, using the elemental correspondences, invoke the sacred energies and bless the sachets. Place them in their corresponding compass point (fire-south, air-east,

Catnip.

water-west, and earth-north). These will keep your home safe for the cat, which can then enjoy the energy and herbs of the sachets.

- Obtain small statuettes (preferably in granite) of kittens. Dedicate these to Bast (or another appropriate cat deity) and plant them in the earth around your domicile.
- Sigillaria unearthed on the site of ancient Tarsus show that an inverted crescent moon was sometimes placed on cat's collars. Presumably this illustrated the cat's connection with the moon, but it could also become a suitable charm for cats today. Set out the crescent in the light of a waxing moon for growing, positive energy, then affix it to your cat's collar.
- If you wish to keep your feline from wandering off, oil or butter its paws regularly. According to Scottish tradition this acts as a talisman keeping the creature close to home.
- To make an amulet, charm, or talisman more powerful for your cat, rub it over the animal's fur. The static electricity positively charges the object for use and attunes the item to that specific cat.

Cat Spells

- If you desire fertility in any form (from pregnancy to a fertile garden), rock a new cat in a cradle as soon as you bring it home. Make sure to state specifically where you want the energy to go or put a token in the crib that afterward becomes a charm to use as needed. If, for example, you wish to conceive, carry the charm near your heart or naval. If you are desirous of a more fertile imagination, meditate with the charm on your forehead over the third eye.

- Egyptian priests sometimes wore a panther tail around their waist during rituals. This token brought strength and safety. Fashion one for yourself out of false fur and wear it when casting spells to improve their potency and support the sanctity of your magical circle.
- In Malaysia, a tiger whisker tied in a man's beard makes his enemies fearful. For a more suitable Western spell, collect your cat's whiskers when they fall out and save them. When you have an urgent need, burn a whisker in a ritual fire and voice your wish, letting the smoke carry it to heaven.

Cat Rituals

- Bohemians take the body of a beloved cat to their fields. They believe that cats are a type of field spirit that can help improve crops. This symbolism might be appropriate for a ritual for a pet that has passed on, returning the creature to the earth so that beauty can grow. Please check any local laws that may restrict this practice, however.

  As an aside, I firmly believe that holding special rites of passage for pets can be very helpful to humans and the spirit of the creature. For most people a pet cat becomes a family member, and saying good-bye is not easy. A ritual helps one integrate and cope with the loss, as well as celebrate the memory of what that pet brought to the home. It also helps prepare the way for new animal companions.

- There is no reason not to perform spells and rituals for your cat when it is ill. Invoke the aid and blessing of a cat god or goddess (see chapter 2). Burn purgative incense such as fennel or sage, anoint the cat with a healthful oil such as rosemary, and provide it with a ritual bowl for a tonic to alleviate its condition (see chapter 5).
- To bless a cat, create a sacred space with your pet in any way suited to your path. Hold the creature gently and sprinkle it with catnip and valerian while invoking an appropriate god or goddess (see chapter 2). Smudge the cat with incense from a sacred fire (a smudge stick is best, as it does not scare the animal). Then thank the powers and take time enjoying your companion.
- Ancient farmers often passed their animals through the smoke of a ritual fire to cleanse them of any sickness and protect them. An easier modern approach is to use a smudge stick or brazier burning with appropriate symbolic herbs. Some options include cedar and pine, which also help alleviate any nasty pet odors!
- Some evidence suggests that the word *puss* originated with the goddess Pasht, a form of the goddess Isis in Egypt. Whenever you create sacred space for your cat, it is perfectly appropriate to call out "Puss" at the center of the circle to invoke the goddesses' blessing and protection.

Egyptian cat from tomb fresco.

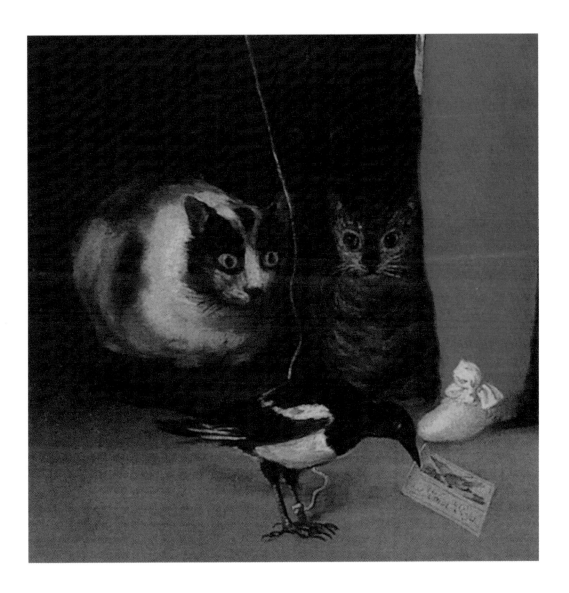

*The cat on your hearthstone to this day presages
by solemnly sneezing, the coming of rain.*
ARTHUR GUITERMAN

FIVE
GYPSY CATS

Thrice the brindled cat hath mew'd.
SHAKESPEARE

Animals from all environ-
ments appear in old sayings
and folk traditions. Part of
this use stems from early animistic
beliefs with reverence for all corners of
nature as having powerful in-dwelling spirits. Part comes from the human dependence

on animals and the belief in animal instincts as being more in tune with universal rhythms and truths.

As one of the most beloved creatures in history, cats are the subject of a wide body of superstition. This chapter explores what some of those beliefs are, how these ideas influenced human discourse, and the ways in which cats were used to foretell the future.

POPULAR SUPERSTITION

Beginning with the beliefs held in common by numerous people, we find cats everywhere from the roadside to the hearth. In some cases the appearance of the cat in itself has meaning. In other instances the person must do something to the cat to entice a result from the meeting. For example, some African tribal traditions say that meeting a lioness is an omen of sterility, yet eating the heart of a lion endows one with the creature's courage and strength.

Rubbing salt on the back of a cat at midnight is said to bring riches. This superstition is likely a combination of three beliefs. The first pertains to salt as a valuable commodity that protects from evil influences, the second has to do with midnight as a magical hour, and the last originates with the cat itself as having mystical power.

Cats influence one's luck. A cat crossing your path on the street brings bad luck, but if you are off the street it is good luck.

Owning a black cat is fortuitous, although meeting one or chasing one away is not. Sleeping with a cat increases serendipity, as does having one on a sailing ship or backstage at a theater. Conversely, on both the ship and stage saying "cat" is taboo.

Opposite: Remedios Varo, Sympatico.

Discovering a cat with double claws is a potent omen of good fortune, even more so than a four-leaf clover. Take good care of this creature and luck will always be with you. In China the older and uglier a cat is, the more luck it brings to its owner. The only cat excluded from this belief is a black cat, who brings poverty and illness when it crosses your path.

Not only live cats influence fortune. Images of cats worn on jewelry encourage good luck and other positive energies. Portraits of lions draw wealth, victory, and strength, for example (see also Chapter 4). This occurs because the ancients consid-

Ancient Egyptian cat coffin

ered many of the great cats to be solar symbols, and so they metaphorically represent the power of light over darkness.

A stray cat coming into your home brings prosperity, especially a white-and-gray one. The only cat for which this is not true is a tortoiseshell, which bears misfortune. Despite the ill luck, other superstitions indicate that this same creature acts as a proof against fire!

Once a cat is in your home, observe it carefully. A cat cleaning itself in your doorway prepares for a visit from the local

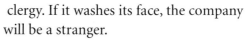

clergy. If it washes its face, the company will be a stranger.

If you want it to rain, sprinkle water on a cat. Closing up a cat in any small area brings unfavorable winds. Conversely, drowning a cat at sea brings favorable winds according to some beliefs, although other sailors feel it draws very bad luck. And speaking of sailors, just possessing a black cat keeps any sailing relatives safe at sea and brings luck into the home. Japanese sailors kept cats on their boats, believing they protect against evil spirits in the sea.

According to some people, because of their connections with magic, cats can see ghosts and purr when they encounter one. This belief stems from the unearthly gleam that happens when light hits a cat's eye. This phenomenon may also explain why some people believe you can tell time by observing a cat's pupil.

In addition to seeing ghosts, cats can become vehicles for human spirits. People in Madagascar believe that cats can carry the souls of the unburied dead. In the Kalahari, Bushmen believe that some lions are sorcerers, and it is not wise to say the word for lion, *n'i,* during the day.

Here are some other interesting cat superstitions:

- If you buy a cat it will be no good at fending off mice. The act of purchasing the cat, rather than letting it find you, deters this ability.

- A lion will not injure a royal prince, thereby showing respect to its equal.
- In southern France, a type of cat called *matagot* is considered the bearer of bad luck, should one come your way. This cat is always black and can be tempted with a chicken. Once captured, place the matagot in a secure container for holding, take it to your home without looking back, and feed it the first bite of every meal. If this ritual is followed precisely, the cat will magically create gold for its owner.

   A slight variation on this superstition exists in Brittany. Here people call the mystical feline *chat d'argent* ("cat of gold"). Apparently this cat can belong to nine people all at once and make them all wealthy.
- If you see a black cat, make a wish before it leaves your sight.
- Fur from a black cat, carried as a talisman, brings improved fortune in gaming.
- Lions have sympathy with leaders, great cats in captivity often dying before a king's demise.
- The Japanese believe that a cat born with a black mark on its back bears the spirit of a departed loved one. This creature is called a kimono cat, and it should always be taken to a temple for protection, lest any ill befall it and thereby the household.
- One should not have kittens or a cat in the house with a newborn. This belief may have originated because

cats seem to like lying in cribs, and people fear a child's accidental suffocation.

- Cats, because of their magical dispositions, have nine lives and always land on their feet.
- In coal-mining regions, people used to keep cats in a cold oven until a new vein of ore was found. This action was thought to help guide and protect the miners.
- The Celts believed that a kitten born in May, if reared, would bring snakes into the house. It would also become troublesome and poorly behaved.
- Some European superstitions claim that a spiritual cat watches over cornfields until the harvest is cut and bound. One sheath of corn from each harvest is saved, being called the "cat." This is returned to the field the next year to bring the protective spirit back again and ensure a good crop. This superstition may have originated in Egypt, where Osiris was the giver of grain and one of his sacred forms was a cat.
- The cat originally gained its gift of second sight by eating the eyes of deceased humans. Thus it has more symbolic vision to use in seeking out the seen and unseen worlds.
- Among certain tribal cultures it is bad luck to marry three times. To avert any troubles the husband should symbolically marry a cat and place a yellow ring of yarn around its neck. After this ritual a third human union will not succumb to ill fortune.
- A cat sneezing near a bride on her wedding day brings good

Louis le Nain, detail from Peasant Family in an Interior.

Opposite: "Wives from Saint Ives" (Mother Goose).

John Tenniel, Cheshire cat from Alice in Wonderland.

luck to the couple and ensures them of many children.
- Never kiss a black cat; it will make you fat. Kissing a white cat makes you lean!
- If you wish to have plenty of silver, Buddhist superstition advises keeping a light-colored cat in the house. If you prefer gold, keep a dark-colored cat.

PROVERBIAL CATS

A good gypsy is not without some flowery phrases to use in captivating other people and in sharing subtle wisdoms. Among such conversational tools we find numerous cat proverbs. One of the oldest known says, "One day as a tiger is worth a thousand as a sheep." This phrase depicts the ancient belief in power and strength as being important elements in effective living.

Proverbs often try to teach lessons in clever ways. For example, a Japanese proverb instructs that it is better to "cover the fish than chase the cat." In other words, one should learn to think ahead. Another proverb from the 1200s reveals the importance of acting on one's desires by saying, "The cat would catch fish if she but wet her feet!"

Cat proverbs reveal some interesting traits in human nature. The saying, "While the cat's away mice will play," talks about how people often behave badly when no supervision is present. Another saying goes, "Beware of the cat that licks from the front but claws from behind," alluding to two-faced individuals.

Other cat proverbs include:

- All cats are gray in the dark.
- A cat with gloves catches no mice.
- A muzzled cat will never catch mice.
- Good liquor makes any cat speak.
- A trapped cat becomes a lion.
- If you play with cats, expect to get scratched.
- A cat and dog may kiss but make no better friends.
- The mouse that accepts a cat's invitation becomes the feast.

PROPHETIC FELINES

Old sayings and superstitions do not limit a cat's powers to mundane life. Indeed, cats are of gypsy blood, effectively prognosticating everything from one's fortune to the weather. People also trusted the cat's importance as a symbol in the diviner's art. Observing "which way the cat jumps" and other feline actions purportedly helps a person predict the future of various matters. Technically this form of divination is called felidomancy.

To know what the weather will be just watch your cat. A cat lying with the flat of its head against the floor is an omen of rain, as is a cat that cleans itself by washing from behind the ear over its face. A cat wagging its tail in winter predicts snow or hail; one leaping around playfully predicts—or invokes—an incoming gale.

A cat scratching a table leg foretells a change in the weather. Egyptians went so far as to say this was the cat's way of raising the winds. If the creature then licks its tail, rain is on the way. Finally, when a cat sits with its back to a fire a storm will soon follow, whereas one scratching frantically on the grass forewarns of an earthquake.

Some cats help people who fish. If a cat runs before you on your way to go fishing, the catch will be quite good. Your efforts will produce nothing, however, if the cat crosses the your path.

Meeting cats in different places and times carries meaning too. Encountering one in the morning on the way to a new undertaking is a bad omen. The only way to avert disaster is to spit after first sighting the creature. Should you meet the cat on the way to church, however, good things are coming your way.

Accidentally walking on a cat's tail brings nothing but bad luck. If a cat leaves your home, it is one of the worst omens, often preceding a death. On a happier note, after a black cat crosses the road, if you are the next person to pass make a wish. If simple enough, your wish should come true within twenty-four hours.

In some settings cats were considered harbingers of death. A cat appearing suddenly, yowling and then disappearing, or a black cat sitting on an ill person's bed, for example, precede untimely deaths. Other indications include a tortoiseshell cat climbing a tree or a black cat crossing a hiker's path at midnight.

An enjoyable type of divination entails posing a question,

Franz Marc, Three Cats *(Düsseldorf, Kunstsammlung Nordrhein-Westfalen).*

then observing any cats nearby. If the cat sits quietly near the questioner afterward, this indicates peace and abundance. Should the cat rub up against the person, this is a positive response that portends very good luck with regard to the question at hand. If the cat jumps in the person's lap, this symbolizes overall improvements soon to follow. Other interpretive values include:

- A cat yawning near you after you voice a query indicates that you should watch for an important opportunity.
- A cat running away from you takes a secret with it. This hidden matter will come to light soon.
- A cat sneezing three times warns of colds coming to family members; one sneeze is fortuitous for your question.
- A cat entering a room you are in with its right paw first indicates a positive answer.
- A cat meowing warns of trouble with regard to your question, especially if any travel is involved.
- A strange cat appearing after you state your question indicates change is on the way; if that cat is black the change is .not a positive one.

THE CAT'S PAJAMAS: INTERPRETING CATS IN DREAMS

Another form of divination by cats entertains the notion that dreaming about these creatures may be an omen of future events.

Examples include:

• Black cats are either good luck or bad, depending on your superstitious background.
• Holding a clean, white cat warns of a situation that although it looks good will only lead to losses.
• Cats on a boat portend improvements.
• Seeing a cat and snake playing together cautions that you could soon find yourself party to a harsh argument.
• A cat attacking you means that enemies are trying to gain advantages over you.
• A leopard in a dream indicates that the future holds success if you do not misplace your confidence.
• Dreaming of lions reveals that you will soon experience tremendous drive toward a specific goal. For a woman, it denotes a new lover on the horizon.
• Taming the lion is an especially fortuitous sign of business success and mental ability. Riding the great cats portends overcoming difficult odds.
• If you succeed in defeating an attacking cat, this foretells wealth and fame. Defeat of a lion or leopard indicates an unexpected victory.

Opposite: ancient Greek symbol of dreams.

Pierre Bonnard,
The White Cat.
(Paris, Musée Dorsay).

• Caged cats, especially the large varieties, portend an unsuccessful attempt by ill-wishers to harm you. You must cope wisely with the opposition for the best possible outcome, however.

- Meeting a sickly cat in a dream indicates forthcoming bad news.
- Hearing a cat in your dream reveals that someone will soon

From medieval Arabic manuscript.

present you with an idea that cannot benefit you. Hearing a lion roar foretells an advancement.

- Being scratched by a cat portends someone else profiting from your efforts.
- Having a tiger advance on you in a dream warns of persecution. If you fend this attack off, however, you will rise above the gossip. If the tiger runs away in fear, your success is unquestioned.

A second type of dream interpretation is based on archetypes of human experience. In this case, the cat and its actions in your dream symbolize something else happening in your life or possibly a person. For example:

- If you dislike or fear cats normally, dreaming about cats reflects unrecognized fears within yourself.
- A beautiful cat may represent creativity or femininity in yourself or another person.
- Cats in general can be emblems of nature's power. They may also represent a figurative rebirth or successful recuperation (the cat having nine lives).
- The animal may depict someone who is being "catty."
- Seeing a cat's eyes or a cat in the moonlight can represent lunar characteristics that need to be explored (for example, the intuitive, instinctual nature).

*Tomb in the
old Jewish Cemetery
of Prague.*

- Because of the cat's association as a witch animal it can symbolize a latent but possibly feared knack for magic and metaphysics.
- The greater cats, such as lions, often represent our animal nature, aggressiveness, leadership abilities, attentiveness, or an overly loud individual full of self-centered roar.
- In Eastern beliefs lions also represent upholding the law in a compassionate manner or heroism. Conversely, in India lions represent divine wrath.

CAT'S EYES: OTHER FORMS OF DIVINATION THAT USE CAT SYMBOLISM

Cats appear as important symbols in numerous settings, including forms of divination other than those previously discussed. For example, in tea-leaf reading finding the image of a cat can mean subversiveness, with the positive outcome of a new beginning. In reading the patterns in coffee grounds the cat represents the need for careful scrutiny and something mysterious.

In the Native American Medicine Cards, receiving the mountain lion represents being thrust into a position of leadership and learning how to use that position wisely. If this card is reversed, it indicates the questioner may have avoided leadership or misused his or her abilities in some way. When the lion roars, it may be to voice conviction or to boast. This is the lesson of the mountain lion.

Card from
The Marseille Tarot.

John Tenniel, Cheshire cat from Alice in Wonderland.

A second card in this divination system is the lynx, a secretive creature that portends the unfolding of mystical gifts to the seeker, especially a keen insight. Reversed, the lynx warns of inappropriate use of knowledge and insight, such as in gossiping.

In the tarot, a lion traditionally appears in the Major Arcana card entitled Strength. This card shows a woman taming a lion, with one hand on its tail. The imagery changes slightly from deck to deck but may have helped originate the saying, "having a lion (or tiger) by the tail." Generally this card represents spiritual power and wisdom to overcome difficult or nearly impossible situations. It also intimates that courage is a necessary component in learning.

Opposite: "Pussy cat, pussy cat, where have you been?" (Mother Goose).

In the *Alice in Wonderland Tarot,* the Cheshire Cat makes an appearance. For those truly devoted to divining for their cats, there is even a *Tarot for Cats.* In this whimsical collection, a cat perched in a tree above a dog is the Moon card, representing the need for your cat to trust its instincts more. The Fool card appears as a cat chasing a bird off a cliff, aptly advising that what appears to be an adventure for your cat will also turn out to be hard work for you!

Chinese astrology features cats as specific personality types. If born in the year of the tiger (1962, 1974, 1986, 1998, . . .), for example, a person is often rebellious and headstrong. Such individuals are predicted to run off on quests or test their personal limits "just because." Additionally, because tigers are natural leaders they often take friends along with them on these risky ventures. Tiger people are wary of others but show a remarkable capacity for intuitive insight.

Although some Chinese calendars replace the cat (1963, 1975, 1987, 1999, . . .), with a hare (see also chapter 2), the lunar symbolism is very similar. Those born in cat years are joyful, fairly honorable, sociable, talkative, and very driven. Whenever possible, cat people like to display their abilities. Cat people remain forcefully independent, which is just as well, as they, like the moon, change with the season. Cats recoup well from setbacks, always landing on their feet, and handle money effectively.

Finally, Western astrology portrays people born under the sign of Leo the Lion as being ruled by the sun. Those born under this sign are said to be bold, noble, devoted, not overly sentimental, ambitious, desirous of honor and pleasure, and good leaders. They have a large roar, expressing themselves strongly, and consequently make enemies (but ones that cannot hurt them).

Leos have financial luck, which is good, as they enjoy luxurious things. People born under this sign do well to look for public positions, such as acting and politics, so they get the attention they crave.

ASTRO CATS: ASTROLOGY FOR FELINES

According to some, the ancient Egyptians so loved their cats that they even explored how the art of astrology could be applied to them, assigning different gemstones and feline personality characteristics to different birth times. The truly dedicated New Age cat owner might want to try this system to better understand a feline companion. A kitten born between March 23 and April 22, for example, can be expected to become a very active and healthy cat that desires a great deal of attention. A good stone to give this cat as a talisman is jet.

If you know when your cat was born, look to the following list for more insights into its behavior and for its lucky birthstone.

Consider using this birthstone as part of an amulet or bonding gift for your cat (see chapter 3).

January 23–February 22: A cat with interests that change with every wind. Have plenty of different toys ready and give it a tourmaline as a charm.

February 23–March 22: A cat that refuses to interact with most people other than its human companion. This creature likes to remain aloof and enigmatic. Give it a malachite as a charm.

April 23–May 22: A cat that loves to play with brightly colored objects and demands a great deal of human affection to be content. Give it a lapis charm.

May 23–June 22: A loving cat, but one prone to whims and changing demeanor. This cat cannot be "owned" by anyone. Give it a piece of coral for a charm.

June 23–July 22: A terminally faithful homebody that is perfectly

Gustave Courbet, detail from The Painter's Studio *(Paris, Louvre).*

content to remain in one place its entire life. Give it a moonstone as a charm.

Lion in medieval astrological manuscript (Bibliotheque Nationale).

July 23–August 22: A very territorial cat that must rule the roost. Befitting this cat's regal demeanor, give it a white diamond as a charm (or perhaps, more realistically, a rhinestone).

August 23–September 22: A very clean, neat, and fastidious cat that will stop to wash itself at the first sign of dirt. Give this cat a rose quartz charm.

September 23–October 22: A cat that wants *lots* of attention and will not take well to other cats competing for your time. Give it a blue topaz as a charm.

October 23–November 22: A perfect cat for a familiar, this creature has incredible instincts. It is also very jealous. Give it a black pearl (or perhaps a black onyx) as a charm.

November 23–December 22: A gypsy spirit surrounded by fur with wanderlust in its soul. Yet this cat can be very devoted if allowed to wander freely. Give it a jade charm.

December 23–January 22: A cat that likes a place for everything and everything in its place. Too many changes disrupt this cat's demeanor until it settles back in. Give it an agate charm.

THE PURRFECT PET

No cat so sweet a mistress owned;
no mistress owned so sweet a cat.
JAMES K. STEPHEN

Many cat owners say that it was not they who chose their cat but vice versa. Indeed, these same cat fanciers believe that their cats own them and often run the house! As a cat owner myself, I must agree. If you are considering getting a pet cat,

*William Hogarth,
detail from Graham
family portrait.*

there are some good guidelines to follow. First, always go to a clean, well-kept pet store or breeder that has been recommended to you by a reliable source. You can get kittens from a neighborhood litter, but there are no guarantees of health with such an acquisition.

Another option is to adopt stray cats or cats who have been left at the humane society. This may save the lives of many cats. A visit to your veterinarian can allay any health concerns about the cat that you may have—whether from a store or the pound.

Second, do not make a quick choice. Look at the kittens carefully. Watch for bright eyes, a good-looking coat, playfulness, and interest in you. A kitten that comes and crawls all over you, one that rubs its cheek glands against you, or one that licks your hand willingly will likely make a good pet. It has already shown its approval of you as a human companion.

Before bringing a new cat into the house make sure no hazardous substances are within paw's reach (even as you might child-proof a house). Watch out for flea control products that can be too potent for kittens; houseplants, including chrysanthemum, lily, mistletoe, philodendron, and English ivy, that are poisonous to cats; garbage that might contain tainted food items; cleaning products that might spill onto the kitten's coat; and most people food. Edibles such as onions and chocolate are bad for cats. If you do have an accident with any potentially poisonous product, call the American Society for the Prevention of Cruelty to Animals (ASPCA) poison control center at 800-548-2423. There is a fee for services rendered.

If you have other animals, expect some difficulties when you bring your new pet home. Cats like to rule the roost or at the very least have the opportunity to do so. That is why several cats in one house tend to fight at first, until they establish a "pecking order" among themselves. It is, however, far easier to introduce a kitten into a house with pets than a full-grown cat. The adult is more threatening to the order already established in the house.

The most influential time in a kitten's life is from six to eight weeks of age. This is when you should handle a kitten regularly to encourage a good social temperament. Play with the kitten, pet it, and get it used to the varying sounds

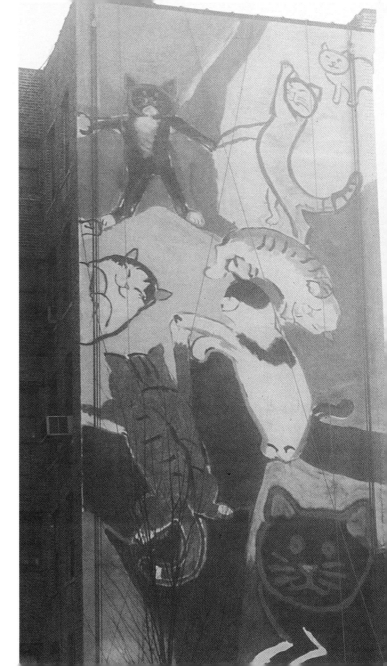

Cat mural (Houston Street, New York).

around your home (such as the vacuum cleaner) for greatest success in integrating the animal with its environment.

TAMING THE LION

It is not difficult to house-train a cat. Keep putting one in the litter box and it will start using it. If it does have an "accident," put the results in the box too as an aromatic cue for the cat. Be diligent about keeping the litter box clean, however. Cats are very fastidious and will not use a dirty litter box. Try adding a little baking soda to the bottom of the pan to help with bad odors.

John Tenniel, from Through the Looking Glass.

On those occasions when a cat sprays to mark its territory in the house, first wash the region with warm water and vinegar. This will cut most of the scent. For washable items add $^1/_2$ cup of borax with detergent to the wash water. Items that cannot be washed need commercial enzyme sprays to really get rid of the scent. Vinegar and warm water will help temporarily, but only the enzyme eliminates the smell completely. One recommended spray is called X-O.

Teaching cats to stay off tables and countertops is sometimes difficult. They love to jump and explore. Two approaches here seem to work relatively well. First, keep a squirt gun handy, using it each time the cat ventures into prohibited areas. Second, scent these areas with ginger, onion juice, vinegar, or oil of rue. Cats do not like these aromas, so they are less likely to explore spots that have been so treated. If neither of these approaches works, try putting double-sided tape in the area where the cat prefers walking—cats dislike the stickiness.

Another ongoing struggle with indoor cats concerns scratching. Most people object to having furniture and woodwork clawed, but for the cat this is a necessary exercise. Scratching removes old claw sheaths to reveal new, sharp claws. It also helps to scent an area.

Having the cat declawed alleviates the problem, but this equates to five amputations per paw. It also places the cat in danger if it should ever escape the safety of the home and can interfere with their sense of balance for climbing and jumping. Instead, scratching posts are recommended, coupled with commercial or homemade repellents dabbed on areas that are off limits. Each time you catch your cat scratching where it should not, take it to the post instead.

Although you do not see this very often, cats can be leash-trained. Begin by attaching the leash to your kitten's collar in the house and letting it walk freely with it in a restricted area. Slowly begin to pick up the leash and walk with the cat, then

move to the great outdoors. Walk the cat in areas away from sudden, loud noises for best results. This step in training is very helpful to cats who always seem to want to sneak out the door.

CAT GOT YOUR TONGUE?

Felines have ways of making their emotions and desires known just as humans do. For example, a cat licking your hand is not simply cleaning you. This actually is a tremendous gift, as it signals the animals' acceptance of and trust in you. Likewise, when a cat rubs its cheeks against you, it is not being simply friendly. That is where a cat's oil glands are located; it is marking you as its human, basically saying to other cats, "Mine."

A cat's ears can help you determine its mood. With ears pointing forward, the cat is relaxed; upright and forward-pointing ears indicate attentiveness. Twitching ears reveal apprehensiveness, and ears flat against the head signal a defensive stance.

When a cat's eyes appear enlarged, this signals the feline's interest in something that either tempts it or frightens it. When a cat's eyes are fully opened, this means it is completely alert. You can often observe this behavior when cats experience new people. It is their way of being wary and observant. If a cat continues to stare directly and shows any other signs of agitation, watch out. A scratch or hiss may be forthcoming.

Half-closed eyes show trust and comfort. Finally, a cat only

Paul De Vos, Cat Fight in the Kitchen *(Madrid, Prado)*

fully closes its eyes when asleep or completely content, such as when being petted for an extended period of time. This behavior may also be seen when you pick up a kitten by the scruff of the neck; in this case it means, "I submit."

With cats the tails do indeed "have it" as the saying goes; the tail is perhaps the most expressive part of a cat's body, exhibiting as many as a dozen different demeanors. A bristly, arched tail indicates defensiveness and a possible forthcoming attack. In females a tail held to one side is a sexual invitation. Aggressive cats often hold their tail straight up and bristle it to look more imposing, whereas one friendly to a human might hold its tail erect and let it shudder slightly.

If the tip of a cat's tail twitches, it likely is irritated with something or someone. Wagging its tail mildly represents a conflict of interest in the cat; it cannot decide on a course of action. The fully lowered tail indicates submission or subjection, whereas one that is stiffly upright with a verticle tip is making a gesture of formal greeting.

Cats do communicate vocally. Loud caterwauling usually indicates an argument, especially if coupled with hissing and howling. Fear is expressed through yowling, and pain by squealing (this sound is very recognizable). Chattering teeth reveal the cat's interest in potential prey. A cat that wants you to follow it chirps, one that is relaxed or passive purrs, and one that wants your attention will "meow" often at your feet.

A little diligent observation will help you interpret what your cat is trying to tell you with numerous other actions. My cat

Kismet, for example, has a favorite pastime that illustrates many communicative behaviors. She sits in the hallway at night mewing to get my attention. When I come near, she rolls over and captures my leg with her paws, showing interest, playfulness, and willingness to submit to me. As I rub her now-exposed belly, she purrs happily until she wearies of the play. She then stands up, rubs against me to mark me as her human again, and finally leaves, her tail proudly in the air.

MICE TO GO

The feeding of a cat can prove confusing to humans. Cats tend to nibble at the foods provided, which usually amount to far more volume than a mouse. After the cat eats the equivalent of a mouse, it leaves to digest its food and may return later for more. To us this appears picky, but it is better for the cat's digestive tract.

If your cat begins nibbling on houseplants or grass, do not panic. This may be a way of supplementing its diet and helping a digestive problem. The grass or leaves clear out hair balls in the intestines, can sooth throat irritation, and add essential roughage to the diet. Just take care with indoor cats that none of your plants are poisonous to them (see page 130).

If you have trouble getting a cat to eat adequately, try moving the food to a quiet, shady area. Cats can be easily distracted, even from food, and a change to a calmer environment might just fix everything. Remember too that if it is overly hot and humid the cat may refrain from food for the same reasons humans do—it can upset their stomach. Periodically also give the cat some variety in what it eats, starting with nutritious dry food from the time it is a kitten. Although the cat may adore canned varieties of food, they are not as good for the cat's teeth and gums. Ask your veterinarian for brand suggestions. And while you are at it, pick up some pet vitamins that can be sprinkled on daily meals. These help keep your cat's body and coat healthy.

ON THE ROAD

Traveling with any animal can be a tricky business. If you plan to take your cat on trips, start getting it used to traveling at a young age by taking it in the car for increasingly long jaunts. There are many types of cat carriers available for travel, one of which should fit your car, your budget, and your cat's preferences.

For air travel, call the airline ahead of time and get details. Some airlines require veterinary papers (shot history and health records), and these are good to carry with you anyway in case of emergency. Mark you cat's cage clearly as a LIVE ANIMAL and make sure the cat has proper identification on its collar. Some cats may accompany you in the passenger compartment with the proper carrier and the airline's permission. The luggage compartment of airplanes is not heated or pressurized. If your cat is skittish, however, consult your veterinarian about possible tranquilizers.

Also call ahead to check your room accommodations to make sure animals are allowed, and under what circumstances. Travel agencies can often tell you what lodges and hotels are pet friendly. Other good ideas include bringing a photograph of your pet in case it should get loose, maintaining your pet's regular feeding schedule as closely as possible to help it adjust, and bringing a few of the cat's toys so it has familiar objects to make it feel at home.

HOME AGAIN, HOME AGAIN

When a cat strays it causes the human owners much worry. It is helpful to know that numerous experiments show that cats have a remarkable homing instinct, however. Although scientists do not fully understand how it works, cats seem to have an internal compass of sorts. So, look around for your feline, shake its food bag, and leave out food and drink. Unless something has gone wrong or the cat is taken in by a good samaritan, it should find its way home.

By the way, the most remarkable illustration of homing occurred in Russia. A cat was sent more than four hundred miles away to live with the owner's mother. After arriving, the cat ran away, making its way back to the original residence in a year's time.

PET CARE

Unless you live in a rural area and are diligent about keeping up with your cat's immunizations, one of the best things you can do for your pet is keep it indoors. Besides the threat of being hit by a car, feline AIDS and leukemia are on the rise. Additionally, indoor cats are less likely to mark their territory or use an unusual location as a toilet, making human life a little easier. Also consider the option of having your cat spayed or neutered. Having a cat "fixed" helps avoid the abandonment

Opposite: "Cross patch, draw the latch, Sit by the fire and spin" (Mother Goose).

of unwanted kittens and putting to sleep of "surplus" cats.

In choosing a health care provider for your pet, look around and interview just as you might for yourself. The prices and outlooks of veterinarians vary just as much as those of human physicians. You need to find someone you trust. Also consult friends with pets for word-of-mouth referrals.

For health care, many human herbal treatments work on animals too, including cats, but in smaller amounts (check with your veterinarian first as some human medications have different effects on or can be harmful to cats). For example, garlic powder, goldenseal, liver powder, fenugreek, and bonemeal mixed into your cat's food or made into a tea added to its water, act as a tonic that also deters fleas. Some cat lovers even use Bach Flower Remedies or color therapy to help their cats.

In the case of flower remedies, honeysuckle is recommended to lift the spirits of a melancholy kitty, and aspen for easily frightened cats. For color treatments, follow this basic guideline, adding the suggested color into your cat's environment wherever possible:

Yellow: for perking up a depressed or listless cat
Blue: for overly frolicsome kitties
Green: to improve your cat's autonomy and confidence
Red: to encourage mating
Gray: to improve your cat's independence
Brown: to keep a cat from wandering excessively

Black: to improve your cat's stamina and focus

Purple: to increase your cat's playfulness and appetite

Rather than buying commercial vitamins, make your own from turkey livers, ends and pieces of vegetables, and cornmeal. Blend and cook until very thick. Serve your cat a little bit daily, again adding garlic if fleas are a problem.

Here is a list of other health problems you may encounter, together with advice on how to deal with them:

Bleeding

Apply pressure to the wound with your hand. If the bleeding does not stop, tie a small piece of cloth above the area and get the cat immediately to a veterinarian. If you cannot reach a professional within twenty minutes, release the cloth slightly, then re-tighten, so that the animal will not lose the limb from lack of circulation.

Breathing

Mouth-to-mouth resuscitation works on cats too. Just take care not to breathe too hard. Remember that cats have a much smaller lung capacity than humans.

Broken Bones

Wrap the animal in a blanket or towel to keep it immobilized, then transport it to a care facility.

Burns

Apply cider vinegar to the area with cool water. Afterward bathe the area in aloe gel, yogurt, or honey.

Little Robin Redbreast sat upon a tree, Up went Pussy Cat, and down went he" *(Mother Goose).*

Constipation

Sprinkle a tablespoon of powdered milk on your cat's food in the morning, and a tablespoon of graham crackers at night. If the condition persists over several days, call your vet.

Diarrhea

Mix $1/4$ teaspoon honey with $1/4$ cup apple juice and let the cat lap it as it wishes. Alternatively feed the cat cooked rice mixed with lean ground beef that is well cooked.

Ear Mites

A drop or two of warm garlic-laden olive oil drowns the mites and also eases itching. Or clean out the cat's ears with a cotton ball soaked in a little wormwood oil.

Eye Rinse

For watering eyes make a tea of comfrey and fennel or celandine. Store in a cool area, discarding the mix when it turns cloudy. Apply 2 drops in each eye twice daily.

Fear

Various conditions can frighten an animal into a traumatic state in which it is not in complete control of itself. Do not move quickly toward it at such times, but speak slowly and calmly. When you can approach the cat, pet it with slow, even strokes until it calms down.

FLEAS

Lavender, fennel, cedar, mint, sassafras, rue, and eucalyptus all deter fleas. Put fresh herbs in your pet's bed, wash its bedding with a final rinse of aromatic oils, comb tinctures regularly into the cat's fur, or dab its collar with the oils to keep fleas away. For indoor treatment wash the floors of your home with water mixed with essential oils or spritz the carpets with any of these oils.

Also add a bit of brewer's yeast and garlic powder to your cat's diet two to three times a week. Always begin flea prevention two to three weeks before the start of the season and continue it two to three weeks afterward to keep fleas out of the house during winter.

GAS

Let the cat eat some angelica, caraway, or fennel.

HAIR BALLS

Give your cat a little vegetable oil or lard. Let it lick it off your hand so that no other foreign substances are introduced.

Heat

If an animal shows signs of overexposure to the heat, wash it with a cool (not cold) cloth and slowly give it water. Do not let it lap up too much water or it will become ill.

Itching

If your cat likes baths, try old-fashioned oatmeal soap to combat the scratching. Or, dab a little warm oatmeal on the affected areas.

Joint Soreness

Rub a rosemary tincture on the affected area.

Poison

If your cat has consumed something it should not have, give it milk blended with egg to absorb the toxin until help can be reached. If possible, take a sample of what it consumed to the veterinarian.

Shampoo (dry)

Mix equal amounts of orris root powder and cornstarch to which any mild aromatic has been added. Brush this through the cat's hair with a palm brush.

Skin Irritation

Dilute thyme or mint oil by half with oil or vinegar and dab it on the sore regions.

TICKS

Apply vinegar, alcohol, or an oil soak to loosen the tick, then remove it with tweezers.

WORMS

Symptoms: dull coat, inflamed eyes, vomiting, cough. Feed garlic and sprinkle food with a thyme tincture.

Caring for your pet at home can be very fulfilling, but there are many circumstances under which you should seriously consider consulting a veterinarian. These include breathing troubles, poor appetite for several consecutive days, injuries where the bleeding cannot be stopped, seizures, diarrhea, odd swellings, and sluggish behavior for more than two days.

By the way, you can now purchase medical insurance for your cat. There are several pet insurance groups in approximately forty states. Ask your veterinarian which group, if any, he or she honors and what types of benefits the insurance offers.

THE TRIVIAL CAT

Cat books are filled to overflowing with pieces of fact and folklore that feline fanciers find fulfilling. This is just a brief sampling for your enjoyment. Share these items with other cat lovers the next time you are at a pet store or in a veterinarian's waiting room!

- Cats cannot see well in total darkness. They use their whiskers, which grow to the width of their body, to give them hints about where they can maneuver safely.
- The wetness or dryness of a cat's nose does not indicate its health.
- Cats have three times better hearing than dogs, being able to hear sounds at 100,000 cycles per second, which is approximately the same level as a mouse's squeak. At a distance of sixty feet they have the capacity to distinguish the sources of sounds that are separated by only a foot and a half.
- Cats cannot always land on their feet. Research shows they need a minimum of just under two seconds' falling time to right themselves.
- Some cats may be fugitives from the law. In Natchez, Mississippi, a cat seen guzzling beer is breaking the law, as is a cat running without a headlight after dark in Dallas, Texas, or a cat that chases a duck on Main Street in Morrisburg, Louisiana.
- The pads on the back legs of a cat act as skid control. They help the cat quickly break off from a fast sprint.
- Cats sleep approximately twice as much as humans. The concept of a "catnap" comes from the fact that cats seem to be able to sleep for short jaunts and awaken fully alert.
- Cats do not always purr in pleasure. When in distress or pain

John Tenniel,
Through the
Looking Glass.

cats sometimes purr because it is nonvocal and does not interfere with breathing.

- The old saying "letting the cat out of the bag" began in the eighteenth century with trickery. Apparently pigs were often transported to market in a bag for easy selling. Some cunning pranksters sometimes substituted a cat for the pig, then neatly ran away with the money. Sometimes, however, the cat put up too much of a fuss and had to be freed. Thus, the con artists were revealed along with their secret.
- With time and patience, cats may be more trainable than dogs as they have a much higher memory retention. One of my cats, for example, taught itself how to turn doorknobs

by grabbing on and swinging. It also taught itself how to use the toilet!

- Most cats live approximately twelve years, which is the human equivalent of being around sixty years old.
- Pound for pound, cats are among the strongest animals on earth.
- A cat's grooming itself does far more than just keep it clean. It improves the insulating ability of the fur by smoothing it. During summer months this protects the cat from overheating.

Grooming removes human scents, the taste of which also helps the cat recognize its human companions even when not in sight. Finally, washing stimulates glands in the cat's skin that help keep its fur waterproof.

- The first cat door was invented by Sir Isaac Newton, who himself owned and loved cats. Knowing that cats always seem to be of contrary mind, wanting to be inside when outdoors and vice versa, he made this ingenious device to make both human and cat life easier.

- Cats are very prolific. According to the noted zoologist Desmond Morris, a single pair of breeding cats, bearing approximately 14 kittens per year in 3 litters, with the offspring similarly fertile, would add up to 65,000 cats in 5 years. Statistics from 1995 showed there are more than 60 million cats in the United States alone.

19th-century advertisement (France).

- The phrase "a cat's chance in hell" originated during the years when hand-to-hand fighting was commonplace. The original saying was "having about as much chance as a cat in hell without claws," alluding to fighting without one's sword.

- Frisky kittens are actually learning important behaviors from their playtime. Each behavior (jumping, batting, flipping, trapping, etc.) is something they would need to know if hunting in the wild.

- Some breeds of cats have misleading names. For example, the Javanese cat never existed in Java, and the Balinese cat was never in Bali. People invented these names to attract human buyers (see also "Breed Beliefs," chapter 2).

- Cats, like humans, exhibit paw preferences. Testing shows that about 40 percent of cats favor their left paw (in humans only 10 percent have this trait). Twenty percent of cats prefer their right paw, and the rest use both paws equally.

CAT.COM

For those readers with access to the Internet who want to learn more about cats, there are several web pages dedicated to our four-footed friends. Try any of the following:

www.catfancy.com: This twenty-four-hour line has information on breeds, several chat groups, news, and a library service.

www.animalnetwork.com: A good all-purpose information web site for all pets, including cats, this site has information on goods that can be purchased on-line.

www.acmepet.com: This web site provides a calendar of cat shows and updates on cat health issues.

www.birman.com: This web site is devoted to birmans. Another good contact is Snowcubs Birmans, 113 South 10th St., Olean, NY, 14760.

www.tica.org: This international cat association provides regularly updated information on its activities.

THE CAT-A-LIST

It's enough to make a cat laugh.
PROVERB

In your interactions with cat owners and breeders and in reading cat-related books, you may come across some unfamiliar terms. Some of these are covered here for your reference. Please note, however, that many other breeds exist than those space allows for listing here.

For more information on the types of cats available, contact local pet searches or check the Internet.

Abyssinian: A breed of cat that began to be recognized in the late 1800s. It is well defined, bearing brownish-red short fur, a medium body build, and large-looking ears.

Agouti: A specific coat pattern in which each hair has bands of yellow, brown, and black.

Ailurophilia: Possessing a love for cats. Conversely the fear of cats is called *ailurophobia.*

Ailurus: A Greek term for domesticated cats. The historian Herodotus is credited with coining the term, having called cats *ailuroi,* which means "tail waver."

Allogrooming: A type of feline behavior in which the cat grooms another animal. Self-grooming is called *autogrooming.*

American Curl: A recently developed breed that has distinctive, roundish ears that stand up on the cat's head looking like satellite dishes.

Angora: A very popular cat breed, possibly originating in Persia and spread by Islamic invaders in the 1400s, when it was noted as a distinct breed in Turkey. This cat has blue eyes, a white coat, very long soft fur, and a graceful appearance.

Balinese: A version of the Siamese breed with long fur. Long-haired kittens started to appear among Siamese cats around 1900. Balinese cats are very dainty and charming, with very graceful movements and a playful demeanor.

Bengal: A breed sometimes called the leopardette due to its distinctive spotted coat, which looks like a leopard's. These are large cats, especially the males, which can weigh as much as twenty-five pounds.

Birman: The sacred cat of Burma, according to legend. These are beautiful cats, with white paws; chocolate-brown legs, tail, and face; brownish-white bodies; and blue eyes. Their fur is soft, of medium length, and often pointed like that of a Siamese.

Boar Cat: An early term for a male cat, later replaced by the affectionate term "tom."

Breeds: Distinctive forms of cats, each of which can be identified by certain characteristics. Some of the most ancient breeds include the Manx, Birman, Persian, and Siamese.

Brindled Cat: A term sometimes used for a tabby, which also has several other nicknames, including "tiger cat."

Burmese: Not to be confused with the Birma breed, this is a short haired cat, first mentioned around the 1300s, with modern notations around the 1930s. It is a small cat with a dark brown coat and yellow eyes.

Calico: A coat pattern seen mostly in females, with white intermingled in a tortoiseshell pattern.

Call Name: This is the name used by a cat owner to literally call his or her pet; a possibly different registered name is used for competition purposes.

Caterwaul: Generally defined as the cry of a cat at mating time, this term has come into popular use to describe any somewhat irritating cry.

Catta: A female cat.

Chartreux: A breed of cat first recognized in the eighteenth-century, but with possibly earlier origins (see chapter 2). It has a bluish coat and orange eyes.

Chinchilla: A coat pattern in cats distinguished by silver fur tipped in black.

Colorpoint: A coat pattern often seen in Siamese cats, with darker fur toward the extremities.

Doe Cat: A female cat.

Felis: The scientific genus for all species of cats. The term likely derived from the word *fe*, "to bear young," alluding to the cat's talent for reproduction (see also chapter 5).

Feral Cat: A domestic cat that has reverted to a semiwild state, exhibiting natural hunting abilities and territorial instincts.

Flehmen: A behavior in cats characterized by a momentary pause followed by sneering expression, which enables the cat to acti-

vate a special organ in the roof of its mouth that enhances its sense of smell.

Foreign: A category of cat in exhibitions, describing a feline with long legs and tail, triangular head, thin body, and large ears.

Gib: An old English term for a male cat. The word *glibert* is also sometimes applied.

Gremalkin: In the 1600s this was a word for an old female cat, and sometimes an old woman too. In the period of the witch-hunts, the term became synonymous with a witch's familiar in the form of a gray cat.

Harlequin: A bicolor cat with 50 to 75 percent white hair.

Haws: A cat's double eyelid, located in the corner of the eye. This eyelid spreads lubrication across the cat's eye. If this part of the eye can be easily seen, get the cat to a veterinarian immediately. It indicates severe illness or malnourishment.

Himalayan: A Persian cat exhibiting Siamese markings, originating with an aggressive breeding program in the 1930s.

Kindle: A term coined around the 1400s indicating a litter of kittens.

Korat: A breed of cat from ancient Thailand, noted as early as the 1300s. Korats have short, dense fur, a medium-sized body, and tall ears poised on top of a heart-shaped face. The Korat's hair has silver on the tips.

Maine Coon: An American breed of large, long-haired cat with a big bushy tail that looks similar to a raccoon's (see chapter 2).

Maltese: This cat originated on Malta, being noted as existing by the 1700s. They have short, blue-gray hair.

Manx: A tailless cat originating on the Isle of Man, having a short plush coat, and long back legs. In its native region, the image of the Manx cat appears on stamps and coins.

Moggie: A nonpedigreed cat (for example, one that is cross-bred or a mongrel).

Norwegian Forest Cat: A breed of cat originating where its name suggests, also known by the fond nickname of "weggie." Some Norwegian stories consider this long-haired, bushy-tailed, impressively large cat as a member of the fey.

Nose Leather: A bit of skin near a cat's nose that bears no fur. The color of this skin helps determine a cat's distinction in pedigree standards.

Persian: An old breed, noted in Persia around the seventeenth century, which became very popular due to its luxurious, soft fur and full tail.

Piebald: A coat pattern distinguished by a predominantly white background with colored patches.

Pointed: A coat pattern characterized by darkening at the extremities (legs, tail, face, and ears). Points are named according to their coloration; for example, seal point is brown and flame point is red.

Puss: A casual name for cats, which may have originated with the Egyptian word *pashr* or the Latin *pusa* ("little girl").

Ram Cat: A male cat.

Scottish Fold: A newer breed of cat bearing distinctively folded ears and a rounded head.

Selfs: Cats who bear solid-colored fur. The hue can vary but no more than one color can be present for this term to apply.

Shaded: A cat's fur is considered shaded if each hair has a dark tip that extends partway down the shaft.

Siamese: Siamese cats appear in literature around the 1300s. They are distinguished by their thin body, blue eyes, angular eyes and ears, and unusual voice. Siamese coats are pointed, growing slowly darker toward the paws, face, and ears.

Singapura: The breed affectionately known as the "Love Cat of Singapore" has a muscular body and short ivory-colored to pale-brown fur. Its face is small and triangular and its tail bears a black tip.

Stud: A male cat kept specifically for breeding purposes.

Superfecundation: When a litter of kittens is sired by more than one father. This occurs because a female cat releases more than one egg at a time and may mate with several males one after the other.

Tom: A term for domestic male cats that originated in the 1700s with a story called "The Life and Adventures of a Cat"; the protagonist's name was Tom. Although the authorship of this story remains unknown, the story was popular enough to influence common language and the term remains in use today.

Tortoiseshell: A coat pattern that appears to be red, off-white, and black, but is actually composed of two colors that mingle to make a three-colored look.

Treading: A cat behavior seen readily in kittens when they nurse. Kneading their mother with their front paws helps stimulate milk flow. In adult cats the behavior continues, often when "nesting" to find a comfortable place to sleep or with a person or animal that a cat regards as its mother figure.

Turkish Van: A breed with origins dating back to the Roman empire, exhibiting long fur, a ring-marked fluffy tail, and reddish-brown fur on the top of the head and tail. Many of these cats have one blue and one amber eye.

Usual: A term used by breeders to identify the customary coat and markings of a specific breed.

BIBLIOGRAPHY

Ackroyd, Eric. *Dictionary of Dream Symbols.* London: Blandford Books, 1993.

Andrews, Ted. *Animal Speak.* Saint Paul, Minn.: Llewellyn Publications, 1993.

Black, William George. *Folk Medicine.* New York: Burt Grankling Co., 1970.

Bleecker, Arline. *The Secret Life of Cats.* Boca Raton, Fla.: Globe Communications, 1996.

Budge, E. A. Wallis. *Amulets and Superstitions.* Oxford, UK: Oxford University Press, 1930.

Clark, Anne. *Beasts and Bawdy.* New York: Taplinger Publishing, 1975.

Cooper, J. C. *Symbolic and Mythological Animals.* London: Aquarian Press, 1992.

de Caro, Frank, editor. *The Folktale Cat.* Little Rock, Ariz.: August House, 1992.

Farrar, Janet, and Stewart Farrar. *The Witches' God.* Custer, Wash.: Phoenix Publishing, 1989.

———. *The Witches' Goddess.* Custer, Wash.: Phoenix Publishing, 1987.

Fox-Davies, A. C. *The Complete Guide to Heraldry.* New York: Crown Publishers, 1978.

Gonzalez-Wippler, Migene. *Amulets and Talismans.* St. Paul, Minn.: Llewellyn Publications, 1995.

Gordon, Stuart. *Encyclopedia of Myths and Legends.* London: Headline Books, 1993.

Gould, Charles. *Mythical Monsters.* New York: Crescent Books, 1989.

Hall, Manly P. *Secret Teachings of All Ages.* Los Angeles: Philosophical Research Society, 1977.

Howey, W. Oldfield. *The Cat.* New York: Castle Books, 1956.

Kieckhefer, Richard. *Magic in the Middle Ages.* Cambridge, UK: Cambridge University Press, 1989.

Knappert, Jan. *African Mythology.* Wellingborough, UK: Aquarian Press, 1990.

Kunz, George Frederick. *The Curious Lore of Precious Stones.* New York: Dover Publications, 1913.

Leach, Maria, editor. *Standard Dictionary of Folklore, Mythology, and Legend.* New York: Harper and Row, 1972.

Lorie, Peter. *Superstitions.* New York: Simon & Schuster, 1992.

Lum, Peter. *Fabulous Beasts.* New York: Pantheon Books, 1951.

Miller, Gustavus. *Ten Thousand Dreams Interpreted.* Chicago: M. A. Donohue & Co., 1931.

Newall, Venetia. *Encyclopedia of Witchcraft and Magic.* New York: Dial Press, 1978.

Opie, Iona, and Moria Tatem. *A Dictionary of Superstitions.* Oxford, UK: Oxford University Press, 1990.

Paulsen, Kathryn. *Witch's Potions and Spells.* Mt. Vernon, N.Y.: Peter Pauper Press, 1971.

Riotte, Louise. *Sleeping with a Sunflower.* Pownal, Vt.: Garden Way Publishing, 1987.

Sams, Jamie, and David Carson. *Medicine Cards.* Santa Fe, N. Mex.: Bear & Co., 1988.

Telesco, Patricia. *The Language of Dreams.* Freedom, Calif.: Crossing Press, 1997.

———. *Victorian Grimoire.* Saint Paul, Minn.: Llewellyn Publications, 1992.

Thomas, Elizabeth M. *The Tribe of Tiger.* New York: Simon & Schuster, 1994.

Thompson, C. J. S. *The Hand of Destiny*. New York: Bell Publishing Company, 1989.

Walker, Barbara. *The Woman's Dictionary of Symbols and Sacred Objects*. San Francisco: Harper & Row, 1988.

Waring, Philippa. *The Dictionary of Omens and Superstitions*. Secaucus, N.J.: Chartwell Books, 1978.

White, T. H. *The Book of Beasts*. Mineola, N.Y.: Dover Publications, 1984.

Williams, Jude. *Jude's Herbal Home Remedies*. St. Paul, Minn.: Llewellyn Publications, 1992.